The
CELTIC LEGENDS
of
GLAMORGAN

The Celtic Legends

of Glamorgan

By
Anthony Rees

With
Illustrations By
Cafall

This book is dedicated to Audrey

"And every night I close my eyes,
But now I've got them open wide,
You've fallen into my hands,
and now you're burning me,
and now you're burning me."

Mike Patton. 1995.

LLANERCH PUBLISHERS,
Felinfach.

ISBN 1 86143 021 3

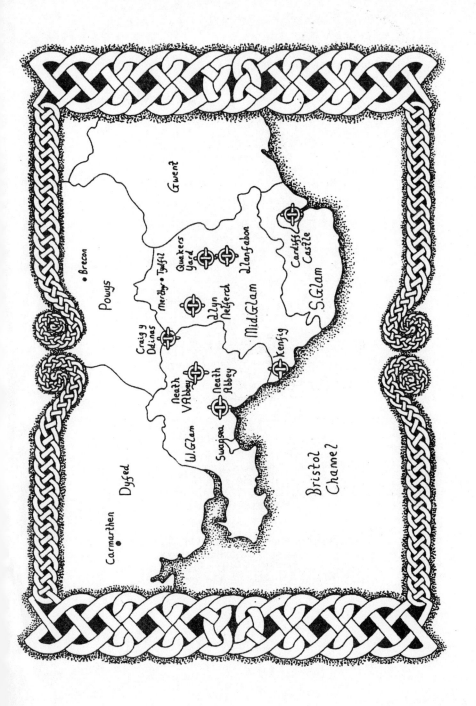

CONTENTS

THE ILLUSTRATIONS
BY CAFALL

PREFACE

Folklore and legends are usually seen as quaint little reminders of how stupid and gullible our ancestors were. The tales are full of fairies, witches, ghosts and magic so they are seen as simple stories to entertain, things that are just not true. This view is an ignorant one and hides the deeper origins and meanings of the tales.

Folklore and legends are undoubtably very odd things. They are not history because nobody can actually prove that they happened but they are also not just shallow stories. If they were simply made up by ignorant peasants to entertain on cold nights then we would expect to find a jumbled mass of stories with no real meanings. On first inspection it does seem like folklore is just a ragged mass of wierd and wonderful tales but, with closer study, patterns and meanings emerge.

This book hopes to show the deeper meanings that lie behind the folklore and legends of Glamorgan. They are not simple stories but the end result of at least a thousand years of Celtic culture in Wales. Nothing exists without roots or a meaning, and the tales in this book have both. They are remnants of a pagan culture and religion that once flourished in all of Britain. The stories have been handed down from generation to generation, for exactly how long we can never know, but enough clues exist to show that the stories are very ancient indeed.

I have rewritten the stories in this book but I have not changed any important parts nor added anything to them except to ease the plots. The artwork has all been drawn by me under the pseudonym of Cafall to complement the stories and is a modern interpretation of Celtic and Saxon artwork.

In writing this book I am indebted to all the people, known or unknown, who took the time to record the folklore and legends. Without them this book would not now exist. I am also indebted to everyone who has helped and encouraged me with my artwork, especially David James, Pamela Constantine, Lorraine at Dalriada, everyone at Keltria, all past and present at Awen Celtic Spirit in Caerleon, Di, Eddie, Ed, Rob, Sean, Chris, Matt, Zob, Mark and my extended family at Trefforest. Special thanks goes out to Fred at Pendragon for all his help and the idea to write this in the first place and to my Nan who got me interested in the past from an early age.

Anthony Rees, Trefforest, 1996.

THE ORAL TRADITION
IN WALES

How some of the ancient legends of Wales have survived the ages is an interesting story in itself. Tales have three forms, they are either spoken and remembered, written down and read, or forgotten and lost. Unfortunately most of the stories from the past have been forgotten and only the wind would know that they ever existed at all. This is mainly because they existed purely in an oral form.

An oral tradition of passing information through the generations by word of mouth exists or has existed in all cultures across the world. In Indo-European culture there was always one class in society who held up this oral tradition. In Irish it was the *fili*, in Teutonic the *scop*, in Hindu the *suta*, in Welsh the *pencerdd* and among the continental Celts it was the *bardos*. Writing is a relatively modern invention in Europe and we have forgotten ourselves what a powerful tool the mind is. The height of this oral culture in our country must have belonged to the pre-Roman Celts.

The Celtic culture of Europe and its survival in Wales formed the roots of Welsh culture and language. The society was mainly a rural one of animal rearing and farming, ruled by a warrior aristocracy. The kings and warriors ruled but knowledge was under the guardianship of the druids and bards. What these people knew formed the very basis for society itself.

The druid's training, all done through the speech of the teacher and the memory of the student lasted for anything up to twenty years. Hundreds upon hundreds of mythological tales were memorised, all full of characters, events and meanings. Added to this were poetry, laws, genealogies and the names and habits of all the animals, birds, trees and elements of the natural world. It is no wonder that people still regard them with awe and mystery.

The coming of the Romans meant that the druids disappeared as a dominant religious class. Their religion was superseded and the bulk of their teachings were lost. This old religion was not totally lost however. Society changes not by a sudden brutal shift but by slow progress and as the Romans merged with the local population so did their religion and ideas. Temples were still built to the Celtic gods and the Romans adopted the local gods. There were still local leaders of Celtic blood and still bards, priests and druids who taught the old ways. The Romans had invaded for economic gain, not to expand the practice of Roman art or mythology. The legionaries could kill the warriors but they could not kill the stories in the minds of the people.

The coming of Christianity affected this tradition very little and in fact saved almost all that we have today. After the Romans had left the people returned to honouring their own gods. The bards and what was left of the druids were free to teach once more. The preachers of the Christian faith sometimes collided with the pagans but the merging of the two beliefs created Celtic Christianity. This form of Christianity had, in order to promote its beliefs, taken the festivals, gods, goddesses and pagan practises and covered them with a thin veneer of Christianity. Through the early writings of the saints and monks we can learn a lot about the pagan faith of Wales.

Saint Gildas wrote in the sixth century about Maelgwn who ruled Gwynedd until around 550 AD. He mentions that Maelgwn used the services of poets and bards in his court. Their function was to praise the king's greatness, spread the word of his power and recite his pedigree and genealogy. By using their awen or poetical inspiration they also aimed to bring some of the qualities of power and honour from the gods onto the king.

These bards survived longer than the Druids and were closely related to the royal houses and dynasties of the dark ages. They were important retainers of customs and traditions but their existence was not continuous. When one of these dynasties died out all the traditions that had gathered around it were lost. The lack of knowledge we have about this period in history is due to these localised dynasties and their dependant bardic communities.

The Irish bard or *ollamh* was required to know at least 250 stories and the Welsh *cyfarwyddion* must have known a similar number. The Welsh Triads which list notable events and people in groups of threes must have been used as a device by which the information was memorised. We have surviving stories about some of the people recorded in the triads but there are hundreds of names about which we know nothing. What was written down was nothing compared with the vast amount of knowledge that has been lost.

After the church in Rome took over from the Celtic church and the Norman kings took over from the Welsh rulers the bardic class had to change continually to avoid becoming non-existent. The Norman lords were eventually won over by the beauty of Welsh poetry and verse and there were still Welsh rulers to patronise the bards. It was not until the sixteenth century that these old Welsh poets totally died out. Even then the poets merely started to write different poetry from the traditions of the past.

It remained for the common people to preserve the legends and tales of the past. Things did not change much in Welsh rural society for hundreds of years. The communities were small and close knit and in the family unit, shops and workplaces stories were passed down from one generation to the other by the word of mouth. These local *y cyfardwydd* or 'familiar ones' were holders of the stories that concerned the local country. The tradition was a living one and tales were added, forgotten or altered but there was also a great deal of conservatism about the traditions of the past.

This knowledge now concerned plant lore, medicine and fairies rather than gods and magic. The material was still rich however, especially on the subject of the fairies.

The fairies are known by a number of names in Wales. There are the *Tylwyth Teg* or 'Fair Folk', and the *Bendith y Mamau* or 'Mothers Blessing'. Different types of fairies exist like the *Bwbachod* who are house fairies, the *Gwragedd Annwn* who are lake fairies and the *Gwyllion* who are mountain fairies. The fairies danced and sang and could either treat you well if you were good to them or treat you very bad if you harmed them.

Other countries have similar lore concerning a magical people. The Isle of Man has the *Fenodyree* or Brownie and the *Sleih Beggey* or Little People. Scandinavia has its elves, dwarfs and trolls and even Yorkshire has the Hob and Robin round cap. These creatures are not the idle fantasies of creative farmers but owe their existence to the old Celtic gods. These gods were not thought of as almighty beings but lived in hills or underground and interacted with the human world, breathing and dying as we do. Over time the memories of these gods, like the Irish *Sidhe* shrank until they became the little people of the fairy world.

The folklore told by the storytellers was also interwoven with the landscape around them. Today we think of landscape as a dead entity that exists to serve our needs or to look pretty. In the past however the stories created places in the landscape that meant something to the people. As these stories were created they also gave to the people a relationship with the land and created the identity of the group, the homeland. The land itself became a living storybook that could be read by the person who knew of its secrets.

A sixteenth-century government report into the activities of the rural population of Wales states that the people used to meet on hills or mountain sides. During these meetings which occurred on Sundays or at holidays the people recited their genealogies and told stories of great battles and the lives of Merlin and Taliesin. The religious revivals in many parts of Wales in the eighteenth and nineteenth centuries put a stop to many of these gatherings but the storytellers still continued their art wherever they found a listening ear.

This link between past and present was very important in giving the people their sense of history and place. The tales were passed on and on until the great change of the industrial revolution eventually broke this continuum in many places. As the cities and towns became populated the people were broken away from their birthplaces and ancestors and so the stories began to lose their meanings. The new societies that formed around these new industries like coal and iron did however still continue something of the old traditions, adding new tales such as those of the mine fairies, the *coblynau*.

In our modern society the land and the past, especially the Welsh past, has lost much of its importance and so fairy tales only exist as curiosities. Oral tradition has succumbed to the succeeding waves of radio, cinema, books and TV. If we listen at all to our grandparents now they have more recent stories to tell us of the world wars or the whirlwind change of society. The old tales of magic and the land don't concern us anymore but they are an important part of the heritage of Wales. They should be remembered so we realise just how ancient and magical this land is and then if we ever do meet the fairies we will at least know how to greet them.

HISTORY OF GLAMORGAN

The Celtic people who first settled in Glamorgan are known only through archaeological evidence. Their traces are found in pottery, metalwork and settlements such as hillforts and homesteads. The hillforts, such as those at Margam, Llancarfan, and Caerau Hillfort in the Ely part of Cardiff would have been occupied from 500 BC to 100 AD. They were the defended settlements or protective enclosures of the early Celtic and pre-Celtic population.

The name of the Celtic tribe which had emerged to populate all of Glamorgan and parts of Gwent is known to us from the Romans. They were called the Silures and lived in the hillforts and settlements of Glamorgan. Their economy was based mainly on the rearing of cattle and sheep and because of this their society was more rural than that of other British tribes. These other tribes would have had larger and more centralised hillforts to control their cereal based economy. The Silures however, like the other tribes, would have probably been ruled by a land-owning warrior elite who engaged in sporadic warfare with their neighbours.

It is when the Romans invade that we have a clearer picture of who the Silures were. The Roman historian Tacitus commented on their dark complexion and curly hair. He thought that this linked them with the Iberian Celts of Spain who had a similar physical appearance but there is a lack of evidence to support this. The Silures probably had their unique physical features because they had merged with this older population. When the Celtic people first came to the area a racially different population of bronze age origins would have been living there. Without large scale Celtic immigration they would have simply merged with this population in what was essentially a secluded part of Britain.

The Romans advanced into South West Wales after conquering the plains of Southern England, in the middle of the first century AD. They met with fierce resistance from the Silures who were a very warlike tribe. Under the governorship of Scapula and then Gallus the Romans advanced steadily through what is now Glamorgan. During this time the Silures fought back using guerrilla warfare to attack the legions' outposts using the advantage of their knowledge of the hilly terrain. In open combat however they were no match for the well organised Roman army. Their hillfort capital of Llanmelin was overtaken and soon enough the first legionary fort in Glamorgan was built at Cardiff.

The conquest of Glamorgan was not complete until 74-76 AD when the whole of Wales came under Roman rule.

After this conquest a well ordered network of forts and roads were constructed to assist in the total subjugation of the native warriors. The legionary fortress at Caerleon in Gwent became the main centre of Roman occupation with other forts at Cardiff, Neath and possibly Cowbridge. An important point to make is that although the population came under Roman rule not all of them actually became Roman.

The capital of the Silures was at Vento Silurium, the modern Caerwent in Gwent, and this town slowly became a Romanised town. The town was watched closely by the nearby Roman army at Caerleon. Eventually the population settled down under Roman rule with tribal councils of the Silures meeting in the town to discuss internal matters. The successors of the old Silurian rulers who had been hostile to the Romans would have been settled in Romanised houses to keep their people under control. The Romans controlled these rulers but the bulk of the population still remained Celtic.

After AD 400 the Romans had officially left Glamorgan and the rest of Britain. Each area now had to defend itself from attack and during this period sub-Roman leaders emerged to rule their lands. These rulers were probably Romano-Celtic in origin and assumed power over their local areas after the Roman authorities left. Not much is known about this period of history which is the darkest part of the dark ages and so we have to turn to the archaeological evidence.

The settlement at Dinas Powys is an important one in Glamorgan and was occupied from the 5th to the 7th centuries AD. This defended site provided evidence of the importing of objects from as far away as North Africa and the Mediterranean. It is an almost unparalleled site in Glamorgan and early historical records tell us that Wales was beginning to be ruled by different local dynasties. Dinas Powys was probably the home or court of one of the early chieftains or kings.

Christianity gradually gained a following from around 400 AD onwards and our main sources for this period are from the legends of saints and martyrs. Saints such as St Cadoc, St Illtud and St Baruc became important figures in the early Celtic church and spread Christianity through their missionaries in Glamorgan. Llantwit Major was the site of St Illtud's monastery and Llancarfan the site of St Cadoc's. Some of our modern churches have their origins in the small buildings where the saints and early Christians first prayed.

St Tydfil is another good example of one of these early Glamorganshire martyred saints. She was born in Wales as the daughter of king Brychan, a local ruler, and she lived as a Christian hermit. She was murdered by pagan Britons around 470 AD and a church was built to commemorate her. The town where she lived still bears the name of Merthyr Tydfil or Tudfil the Martyr and her shrine still existed in a church here until recently.

A succession of kings ruled over the area of Glamorgan, defending it against attackers such as the Vikings who decimated large areas of land in 988 AD. The Saxons were also making great gains in Britain and eventually the Welsh kings were the only surviving Celtic rulers on the British mainland outside of Scotland.

The end of the kingdom of Glamorgan started with the death of Caradoc ap Llewelyn in 1081. The Welsh kings of Glamorgan could no longer survive independently from the advancing Normans and were slowly annexed into a greater England. At the end of the 11th century the Norman Robert Fitzhamon invaded Glamorgan and defeated its ruler Iestyn ap Gwrgant. After this there was no large scale Anglo-Saxon settlement in the area but much of the local Welsh population moved upwards to the border vale of Glamorgan.

Welsh rulers still did exist in Glamorgan for the next few centuries. There were still local Welsh lords and the rising of people like Owain Glyn Dwr, who liberated Glamorgan in 1402, meant that the old Welsh culture continued in a haphazard way. As the Normans and the Welsh merged into one population the two cultures mixed and gave us new versions of old legends such as the romantic chivalry of the French Arthurian legends. A new Welsh culture also emerged and soon enough the Normans were employing Welsh bards in their own service. We leave the history at this point because most of the legends and tales were now surviving in the folklore of the common people.

THE SOURCES
OF THE TALES

The stories in this book come from a variety of different sources. Because the stories were originally part of an oral tradition we cannot be sure of the exact origins of the tales but some of the material is undoubtedly very old. It is only through tales that were written down that we have evidence of the early Celtic legends and mythology. The oral tradition that once carried Celtic mythology has since died out, meaning that a lot of the stories have been forgotten. This transition from oral tradition to written record occurred in a number of ways.

The majority of the fairy stories come from the early work of scholars in the nineteenth and early twentieth century. John Rhys, a professor of Celtic at Oxford, collected many stories in his book on Welsh and Manx folklore. Likewise Wirt Sykes collected stories from the local population and published them. The Reverend Elias

Owen also collected folklore in North Wales at the end of the last century. To these early scholars we owe a lot for their ramblings around the countryside of Wales brought to light and preserved a rich vein of Welsh folklore.

As so much folklore has been forgotten in the last two hundred years these late sources preserved what was stored in the minds of the Welsh storytellers. Other scholars collected tales from Scotland and Ireland and here they found that lengthy tales still survived in the oral folklore. By the time Welsh folklore was written down almost all of the long tales of heroes, gods or magic had disappeared and mainly scraps remained. Rhys himself regrets that he did not start collecting folklore years earlier for he was all to aware of how quickly it was dying out.

The work of these early scholars has been continued up to recent times by modern folklorists such as Robin Gwyndaf. As curator of the Welsh Folk Museum in the 1960s he collected 600 hours of sound recording and over 18,000 items of narrative from the Welsh people. Trefor Owen also collected important pieces of Welsh folk customs in the 1950s. The tales that survived at this time were mainly short local legends but they were still full of fairies, devils, witches, magicians, ghosts, dragons, winged serpents, black dogs and water monsters.

The sources of these scholars were the Welsh people themselves. These storytellers were mainly from the older generation, having heard the tale from their parents or grandparents. It was these tradition bearers that kept the stories alive and it is thankful that at least some of their testimonies survived after their deaths. Unrecorded folklore tales are probably still being told in the farms and houses of Wales but these are disappearing with the passing of each day.

The other major source is from ancient documents. The Mabinogion, the best collection of ancient Welsh legends was written down in two manuscripts, The Red Book of Hergest and the White Book of Rhydderch. Both of these date to the thirteenth century but the origins of these tales are much older than this. The earliest manuscript fragments of the stories are dated to around 1225 but the motifs and events in the stories point to a relationship with an older oral tradition. The story of Gereint and Enid that I have used is one of the later romantic tales in the Mabinogion but it still has older associations.

Another source I have used is medieval religious writings. Gerald of Wales, a clergyman went on a tour of Wales in the twelfth century and recorded a fairy tale from Neath. He acted like the scholars of today in recording a piece of local folklore and from this we can see that the form of the fairy tale in Wales has remained almost unchanged for 800 years. From the Life of St Collen preserved in the Hafod 19 manuscript of 1536 there is also a tale relating to how a saint overcame the king of the fairies in the sixth century AD.

For interpreting the meanings of the tales I have used the wealth of other Celtic material that has survived in written form. The vast amount of Irish mythology is used as a basis for drawing many of the parallels. Most of these tales date from around 1000 AD but draw from earlier manuscripts and oral sources. Some of the events and societies described may even date back as far as from the time of the birth of Christ and have their roots in prehistory.

The other sources include works such as Geoffrey of Monmouth's *Life of Merlin* dating from 1150. Ancient Welsh poetry is also valuable as some of it dates from as far back as the 6th century and mentions many figures from Celtic myth and legend. There are other useful pieces such as Scottish and Breton manuscripts, the Welsh Triads and the large amount of Arthurian legends whose origins lie in Celtic myth.

The written material from the Celtic countries of Wales, Ireland, Scotland, Brittany, Cornwall and the Isle of Man as well as certain stories from England are all important in discovering Celtic mythology. In using these sources I have tried to give a more fuller meaning of the legends found in Glamorgan. To view them independently on their own would be foolish and would mean ignoring the whole range of other sources that can be examined to gain some meaning from these strange tales. Celtic myth and legend is a very rich subject, both in terms of artistic beauty and inner meaning, and the county of Glamorgan is as rich as any other area in this respect.

Arthur sleeps

To rise again

KING ARTHUR
IN THE CAVE

King Arthur, Britain's famous legendary king, has a myriad of associations with Wales. Arthur as a figure of myth or history has been placed all over Britain in many roles, from a semi-Roman leader to a semi-French chivalrous knight. The Welsh have always kept him close to both their hearts and their land and he became a symbol of Wales's Celtic past and identity. Welsh people are truly adamant that Arthur walked and breathed in Wales.

It is quite fortunate then that evidence of Arthur's involvement in Wales is overwhelming. His earliest Welsh literary appearance is in the Book of Aneirin in the late thirteenth century and he makes many appearances in the famous legends of the Mabinogion. These legends name Caerleon as his court and sometime after the Romans left Britain the overgrown amphitheatre became known as 'Arthur's Round Table'.

Glamorgan has an equally important legend relating to Arthur's last resting place. Three caves, all called Craig y Ddinas, have claims to be where ancient Britain's last great

27

king is sleeping, one near Llantrisant, one in Ystradyfodwg and one near Pontneddfechan. The cave with the best claim and the best legend is the one near Pontneddfechan in the Vale of Neath. This is the story that I shall relate here:—

"King Arthur had defeated the Saxons for a final time at the long and devastating Battle of Camlann, around 539 AD. He was travelling to rest at one of his strongholds in Wales. With him were what was left of his army and a retinue of knights from his fair court. Owein, Cai, Gwalchmai, Peredur, Geraint, Trystain, Bedwyr, Cilhwch son of Celyddon, Edeyrn and Cynon all rode alongside him.

Arthur was exhausted after the gruelling battle but refused to rest, no matter how hard his companions pressed him to. He rode high in his saddle but his face showed the strains of weariness and his body was covered with many bloody wounds. When evening came he finally stopped at a sheltered clearing in the forest by the side of Craig y Ddinas, which means 'The Rock of the Fortress'.

Some knights and soldiers went to the woods to hunt for their supper but most of the army set up their camp and went to sleep. By twilight all of Arthur's war band and the great leader himself were immersed in the deepest of sleep. As it began to get dark a mist spread from the head of the valley and began to float down towards where Arthur was resting.

In a nearby village an old Wise Woman saw the mist rising and with her magical sight she could see that it was

28

not formed naturally. She ran wildly from house to house around the village crying that a witch was coming and that danger would follow. The villagers came running out of their homes but after they had seen the cloudy mist, which was quite a natural sight after a hot day, they ignored her and went back to their suppers.

The old woman however knew that it was another white witch she could see. After gathering up her charms she headed out in the direction of the pure white mist. The mist was getting thicker and thicker in the forest but she soon stumbled onto the clearing where Arthur's war band lay sleeping.

She could hardly believe her own eyes as her gaze rested on the sleeping figure of her king. The mist soon became so thick that it smothered Arthur and his knights in a white cloud. The woman hid behind a hazel bush and waited.

Soon the mist obscured even the bright full moon but the Wise Woman could see the knights faces glowing with a ghostly white light that emanated from their pale, death like skin. A trance gripped her as she gazed at the face of her king and she was unable to even move a finger, not wanting to look away from his noble visage for even a moment.

Arthur's features were replaced by the glowing face of the sun as the woman was woken up by the bright morning. She cursed herself for falling asleep and looked quickly over to where the king had lain. She could no longer see the bodies of men but where Arthur had been sleeping was an opening to a large cave. As she continued to watch in disbelief the grass around the rocky entrance seemed to grow over and the cave soon disappeared without a trace.

Sorrowful that her king had been taken by magic she returned to the village in tears telling her story to everyone she met.

"Arthur the king is imprisoned", she screamed, but no-one believed her story, everyone had heard that Arthur had died in battle. The woman must have simply gone mad.

Hundreds after hundreds of years passed. The Wise Woman died taking her hopes of seeing Arthur freed into her grave. The village grew into a town and the forest surrounding the clearing was cut down to build houses and provide firewood for the town that sprung up close to Craig y Ddinas.

A Welsh drover taking his cattle from West Wales passed through Craig y Ddinas. As the cattle drank in a stream he cut a hazel branch to fashion into a walking stick for the long journey to London. When he reached London he sold his cattle and stood on London Bridge to admire the magnificence of the River Thames and the large city. His hazel stick had miraculously survived the long and arduous journey whilst those of the other drovers had been reduced to splinters.

He rested on it and resolved to take the charmed stick back to Wales with him for the next drove. As he was admiring the scenery a strange man walked up to him and inquired as to where he had got the stick. The drover asked him what business it was of his.

The man replied, "I have dreamt of the tree which that stick is a part of, I have dreamt of something wonderful to be found near it, you must take me there". The drover looked at the ragged old man strangely, disbelieving his wild claims.

"It will lead you to great riches", the old man added, and the drover, slowly realising that the man was a wizard, agreed to show him from where he had cut the stick.

The two men set out and soon reached the hollow where the hazel bush stood. The drover dug into the earth where the old man directed and soon came across a thin stone slab. With great effort he pulled it away and revealed a stairway leading deep into the earth.

"Follow me" the wizard instructed and they descended down the stairs. At the bottom of the stairs there was a small gold bell suspended from the ceiling. "Do not ring that bell, never!" warned the old man and he continued ahead of the drover down a dark passage.

The passage went on for about fifty yards and at the end of it they found a large cavern and were astonished to see what was inside it.

Lying in a circle on the floor were hundreds of soldiers, their swords lying on one side and their round shields on the other. Inside this circle were twelve knights, all dressed in the best quality shirts and trousers and each lying on a different coloured cloak. At the centre of these two circles lay a tall noble-looking man.

He was brilliantly adorned in a red silk shirt covered by a fine chain mail shirt and a brilliant crimson cloak. By his right side was a huge bejewelled sword that glinted in the light of three lamps that lay around it. A large red enameled shield displaying a white cross on it lay at his left and his finely-featured head was crowned with a glinting polished gold embossed helmet.

"That is our King, the great Arthur!" The old man said to the bewildered drover.

"Those men around him are his twelve greatest knights and lying outside them are their armies, all are waiting for the day that they are needed once more to rise up and protect our country from desolation. When the Black Eagle and the Golden Eagle clash the force will shake the very earth and ring the golden bell, then Arthur shall rise again. He will defend us as he has done before and drive away the enemies of the Welsh. His court will be established at Caerleon once more and he will rule justly over the islands of Britain".

The wizard stood gazing at Arthur for a long while. When the drover started to wonder about the huge cave the wizard led him to two piles of coins, one gold and one silver lying by the side of the sleeping knights.

The wizard looked deep into the drover's eyes and said "These are the riches, you may take the gold or the silver but never both at the same time". The wizard paused, then continued, "and do not ring the bell, if you do one of the knights will awaken and ask if the time has come for them to rise. If this happens you must say The time is not yet upon you, sleep awhile and you must say it immediately".

The wizard began to leave the cave as the drover fell upon the pile of gold coins, "I have no need of riches", he said, and the drover saw him no more.

The drover made many visits to the cave and became very rich. One day he did brush against the bell but remembered to say the correct words to the questioning knight. This happened a second time as he became more careless in his greed but he simply told the knight to sleep on.

On the third visit however the drover became much too greedy and weighted himself down with entire sacks of gold. He jangled so much that he failed to hear the bell when he brushed against it. Within moments he was surrounded by angry knights who dragged him into the centre of the circle and beat the thief to within an inch of his life.

When he came to his senses he found himself bruised and battered in the grassy hollow and could find no sign of the cave entrance. He dug and dug for months to find the entrance, but never found it again. His health failed him after the beating he had received and he died a poor man, never to see Arthur or his gold again. No one has seen Arthur's cave since."

The sleeping hero in other cave legends is not always Arthur, sometimes it is the Welsh prince Owain Glyndwr, who united Wales early in the fifteenth century. Alternatively it is Owain Lawgoch (Owain of the Red Hand) who was a thorn in the English's side for most of the fourteenth century. All of them are heroes of the Welsh nation and are not dead but are said to lay resting, waiting for the time that they will arise again.

Across the sea Finn, the great Irish hero, is also said to

be sleeping with his warriors waiting to rise up once more and save Ireland from tyranny and oppression. Maybe in an even earlier version of the story the figure in the cave was a Celtic god, waiting to save his tribes in their hour of need.

The cave in which Arthur sleeps seems to have quite some legendary importance. It is the site where Arthur was reported to have killed terrible giant called Garwed. The giants name may survive in the place names of Ynysarwed and Abergarwed which are in the same area. The giant's body was also buried under the rocks of Craig y Ddinas.

A megalithic tomb in Gower also has a strange association with the Glamorgan cave and Arthur. When Arthur travelled towards the Battle of Camlann he also passed through Craig y Ddinas and got a stone lodged in his boot. With great annoyance at the distraction he picked it out and threw it away. So great was his strength that it landed on top of Cefn Bryn in the Gower peninsula to become the capstone of the tomb, which is called to this day 'Arthur's Stone'.

Obviously the 4000 year old tomb was not formed in this way but such tales as these enriched the links between the land and the people who inhabit it. This tale of Arthur sleeping is not something that has been invented recently, it has been told for hundreds upon hundreds of years, becoming a very important part of Wales' identity. It must have been quite a comforting feeling for a people who were constantly invaded to think that Arthur was out there not very far away, waiting for the day that Wales most needed his protection!

GLAMORGAN'S
MERLIN

Everybody has heard of Merlin, Wales's most famous magician. He was a prophet, a seer, a poet and a madman. He is credited with discovering the White and the Red Dragon that battled beneath Dinas Emrys in North Wales, the Red Dragon ultimately being the victor and becoming the national emblem of the country. Most of the tales about the Welsh Merlin take place in North Wales but he still has his associations with South Wales. In Geoffrey of Monmouth's *Life of Merlin*, written in the twelfth century, he is described as giving a code of laws to South Wales and of predicting the future for its leaders. More importantly we find, in Glamorgan, the curious tale of Twm:—

"Twm lived near Kenfig Pool. His father or his father's father had been a skilled and acclaimed poet and Twm inherited some of this gift. His skill however was not in the magic of words but in the power of the future for

Twm was born a prophet. His ability to predict the weather and the changing fortunes of the land made him an invaluable help to his farming fellows and his fame grew as he did.

Soon enough his fame spread farther and farther. Eventually the local lord overheard one of his servants talking about this 'fortune teller'. He thought it would be an amusing event to bring him into his court and see if his predictions came true. Twm was sent for, but being a wise man and not willing to use his powers for mere entertainment he refused. This angered the lord considerably and he had Twm arrested and thrown into jail until he would comply with his request.

Twm stayed there for a while, not opening his mouth to speak for anyone until one day he asked to see the lord. He was brought out in front of the court and told to give a prophecy.

'Your baby son will die', he said solemnly to the lord. The court fell dead silent at this surprising judgement. The lord suddenly burst out in laughter, 'How can he die when he is looked after by the best midwives in the land?'

Twm only stood there and repeated his prophecy.

'You are a fool!' the lord exclaimed. 'Take him back to the dungeons; he may learn some sense from the rats!' The court erupted in laughter and Twm was taken away once more.

That night the lord's son was put to bed as usual but by the morning the baby was dead, strangled by his apron strings while he slept. The lord was grieved and wished he had never set eyes on Twm. Ordering Twm released he banished him from his lands so as not to be reminded of his own laughter at the sorrowful prophecy.

Wandering about the countryside Twm supported himself by begging, labouring and receiving odd favours for his prophecies. Soon after the lord died, however, and he was able to return to his home.

One day upon entering a village he was met by an obnoxious lad who taunted him for his magical powers. Twm shut his eyes and entered a prophetic trance.

'You will die three times before the night is out,' he said, at which the rest of the village laughed.

'Dying three times is impossible,' they said, and Twm was thrown out of the village.

That evening the obnoxious boy was climbing a tree in search of bird's eggs. He was bitten by an adder in the tree, lost his balance and fell, breaking his back on a branch and falling in the River Kenfig to drown.

Thus he had died three times as had been foretold. After this Twm was respected by everyone and his fame as a prophet meant he never had to beg for food or prove himself again."

You may be wondering what all this has to do with Merlin. If we look at Geoffrey of Monmouth's *Life of Merlin* we find a very similar incident occurring in this ancient book which draws on even earlier sources. The prophesy of Twm is the same prophesy foretold by Merlin:

"After witnessing (and some say causing) a mass slaughter at the battle of Arfderydd in 573 A.D. Merlin went mad and has been living like an animal in the forests. At this point in the story Merlin has been imprisoned by King Rodarch of North Wales for his own safety. Chained and bound in the castle the sorrowful Merlin wants nothing more than to be released to face his torment alone in the wild forest.

He cannot bare to speak to anyone and only gibbers to himself while he is held in the castle. One day however the king's wife arrives at the castle. As she is greeted the king kisses her and absent mindedly plucks a stray leaf out of her hair. As it drops to the ground Merlin bursts out laughing.

He is hard pressed by the king to reveal why he was laughing but Merlin refuses to explain himself. The king promises him gifts and riches if he will account for the outburst but Merlin wants only to be free to return to the forests. The king is intrigued so much by Merlin's behaviour that he gives in and releases him. Merlin then explains that he was laughing because the king had treated the leaf as if it were a mere annoyance when it had meant something much more important.

He tells the king that the queen had been lying in the undergrowth with her lover when the leaf had become entangled in her hair. The leaf had betrayed the queen but the king was too blind to see it. The king starts to curse his wife but she only smiles and questions his judgement for believing such a madman. She proclaims her innocence and says that she will prove to her husband that Merlin is wrong and that her chastity is clear.

She calls over one of the young boys of the court and

she asks Merlin: 'How will this boy die?'

Merlin answers, 'When older the boy will die from falling from a cliff'.

Secretly she then tells the boy to go and change his clothes and cut his hair. When the boy returns in this disguise she asks of Merlin: 'What of this boy?'

'This boy will meet a violent death in a tree when he has grown into a man,' he answers.

The queen again whispers to the boy to go and dress up as a girl. When he returns she asks for a third time: 'How will this girl die?'

'I do not know whether she is a girl but she shall die by drowning,' Merlin said.

Turning to her husband she asks whether he needs any more proof of Merlin's madness. How can the same boy die three different deaths?

The king accepts that it must have been a lie, he apologises to his wife and Merlin is freed to wander wild in his forest.

Many years later when the boy had turned into a man he went out hunting. Seeing a stag he urged his horse and dogs forward to chase after it. The stag bounded effortlessly over the fields and hills, always keeping just ahead of the hunter. In the excitement of the pursuit he become careless and ran his horse too fast over a hill. Losing its footing the horse pitched off the cliff and threw the rider off its back. As he plunged off the cliff the boy's foot caught on the forked branches of a tree, his lower half hung into a stream and he died, fulfilling the prophecy of the triple death".

This triple death prophecy is also repeated in the twelfth century Scottish manuscript *The Life of Saint Kentigern,* where Lailoken, a similar figure to Merlin, also goes mad and lives as a wildman in a forest. It is Lailoken himself who dies the triple death that he has prophesied, by cudgelling, piercing and drowning in the River Tweed in southern Scotland.

In the legend of another 'wildman' called Suibhne Geilt it is a Christian, St Moling, who gives a prophecy of a death similar to Twm's. The saint says that Suibhne's murderer will die by a weapon, burning and drowning. The man is soon enough wounded by his own spear while climbing an oak tree, he falls off into a fire and drowns in a river while trying to extinguish the flames.

The image of the threefold death itself is not however just a magical oddity invented to make an interesting story. It is found in a number of myths and legends and its origins may go back to the very roots of Celtic civilisation. In the Celtic literature of Ireland King Diarmait, a sixth century king, is speared by an enemy, his house is then set on fire and as the king tries to escape the flames he drowns in a vat of ale.

Further evidence is found in Wales. In the Mabinogion tale of *Math Son of Mathonwy* the hero Lleu could not be killed by normal weapons on land or sea. For him to be killed three conditions had to be met, he had to be hit with a special spear while standing with one foot on a tub of water and the other on the back of a buck goat.

A preserved body found in a peat bog, dubbed Lindow Man, may also hold physical evidence of this practice. The body is dated to sometime in the first century A.D. and was found at Lindow Moss bog near Wilmslow. The man, who's hands were tied, had been bludgeoned on the head, hanged and also had his throat cut. This would be a case of 'overkill' if it were not for the evidence of legends like those of Merlin, Lailoken and Twm.

The number three was considered a magical number by the Celtic peoples. Throughout the myths and legends three occurs as a magical number and gods and goddesses exist in triple form. The Welsh bards also used to memorise hundreds of tales using the Triads which were long lists of events and people grouped into threes.

The triple death tales might relate to an earlier form of ritual sacrifice to placate the triple powers of the gods. Otherwise it may just relate to the high esteem given to triplicate events, with a triple death occuring as the obvious conclusion to a person's mythological life. It is natural therefore that the prophets, saints and druids would have the ritual power to prescribe this fate to others.

The fact that the threefold death motif survives in the tale of Twm of Kenfig several hundred years after Geoffrey's book was written and nearly two thousand years after Lindow Mans death is very interesting indeed. The survival could be because the tale was taken from the thirteenth century *Life of Merlin* manuscript and retold by someone who decided to place it in Glamorgan. This seems unlikely; there would have been a few academics in Glamorgan a century ago able to translate the story from its Latin original, but why would they wish to introduce it to the peasantry of Kenfig in the first place? The answer for

41

this survival of an idea must be that the folktale of Twm is a watered down remnant of a once powerful legendary figure similar to Merlin. These tales would have been told a millennium ago in Glamorgan and their roots reach back into distant prehistory. What form the original legends took we will never know but Twm of Kenfig is still a very important legend to be found in the supposedly Anglicised coastal area of Glamorgan.

THE REVENGE OF
THE FAIR FOLK

The setting of this story about the fairies is in the parish of Merthyr Tydfil at a farmhouse called Pantannas near Quakers' Yard. The name Pantannas might mean 'Hollow of the Legend,' which would relate to this sorrowful tale, or alternatively 'Hollow of the Staying' because the river sometimes flooded and became impossible to pass. The area is full of stories of the fairy folk, and archaeological remains, and another story in this book *The Llanfabon Changeling* is set close by. The stories are unusual in their completeness, and came from a Mr Craigfryn Hughes, one person whose memory was thankfully not lost.

In this tale the Fairy Folk are not the cute little characters that most tales would have you believe. They may dance and sing and leave pure gold in exchange for the odd drop of milk, but sometimes they show their harder

43

side. There are many tales describing what happens when the sanctity of the fairies way of life is broken or if they are treated disrespectfully. When happy they are very merry, sweet things, but when they are wronged their fury can fall hard and fast, or rather hard and slow as this tale shows:

"Long ago there lived a farmer who harboured not a piece of love for the fairies. He would lie in bed at night, tossing and turning as the noise of their revelries drifted across the fields of Pantannas. Most nights they would be at it; singing, dancing, playing the harp and flute all through the night until just before the break of day. Most people would have found this a wonderful experience, falling asleep to the gentle sound of fairy song, but not the farmer.

He was a sour-tempered man, especially at this harsh time of winter, and would shout at the fairies from his window, calling them rude and vulgar creatures. He tried everything to get rid of them. One night he even ran towards them in his night-gown shouting and flailing his arms. They would disappear from their fairy rings, but as soon as he left they would just come back and laugh all the louder.

After trying everything to make them stop their nocturnal gatherings, he had reached almost the end of human despair. Many more sleepless nights were to be had until an old witch happened to hear of his plight. She herself hated the fairies, being as sour of mind as the farmer, and in return for a day's worth of milk from his cows, she agreed to show him how to get rid of them.

Her advice was this: That the farmer should arise the next day before dawn and set to work ploughing all of the fields that the fairies frequented for their midnight revels. Once all of the fairy rings had been destroyed and all they had left to dance upon was the bare ragged earth they would surely trouble him no more.

The farmer woke the next morning and did as he was counselled. As he drove his plough and horses over the dark fairy rings he whistled for the first time in his life, though it was not a pretty tune. Soon enough a large part of his farm was coloured a deep harsh brown by the furrows of bare earth.

That night he slept soundly, not as a result of his hard day's labour but because the fairies did not come. He was untroubled by them throughout the rest of the winter and where there had been fairy song in abundance was now covered in a blanket of silence.

When spring came and threw the last throes of winter off the land, still not a single whisper or pluck of a harp was heard, even the birds were silent. The flowers bloomed late that year and their colourful hues were dulled, but the farmer was not a person to notice things such as this. He went about his daily business of sowing and planting the barley and wheat, glad that he was getting sleep at night and not suffering from the fairies' joviality.

One late spring evening when the air was crisp and clean, the farmer was walking through his lands, almost enjoying the sweet-smelling air and the sight of the deep lush green hills spread around him. He stopped dead in his tracks however as a small man appeared before him. The figure, which hardly reached up to his knee, was wearing a red waistcoat so deep in colour that it was the same shade as the crimson sky overhead.

The figure brandished a short but menacing-looking sword. Pointing it at the astonished farmer the fairy sneered:

'Vengeance cometh, fast it approacheth!' then he was gone as fast as he had appeared.

The farmer was a little troubled by this and went to sleep that night expecting the fairies to come back to the fields, which had regrown their covering of grass, and sing and shout louder than before.

After a sound night's sleep he woke the next morning to the sound of the cockerel and chided himself for fearing such a small man. A few more uneventful days and nights passed and he almost forgot about the red man altogether, but one night as he lay sleeping he was awoken violently. It was not the fairy song that woke him but a violent trembling that made the whole house shake from its foundations. As he lay cowering in his bed a voice boomed out from the night sky:

'Vengeance cometh!' Then the trembling stopped and all was silent.

The farmer could do nothing but shiver beneath his sheets for the whole night. He left his house in the morning bleary eyed and half expecting to meet the red fairy on his doorstep, but what he saw was much worse.

His fields that had been sheets of bright green and

yellow the day before were now all blackened from fire as colourless as a moonless night.   Walking around in this absolute destruction, he knew it could only be the fairies who were responsible.   A whole year's crop had been destroyed and he faced almost certain ruin.   He began to curse himself loudly for having taken the witch's advice.

'Your curses will avail you not!' a voice said from behind.   The farmer turned to see the same crimson-garbed fairy pointing his sword at him once again.

'It only but beginneth!' he said bitterly.

The farmer on hearing this, not being a very strong or proud man, broke down in tears instantly.   He fell to the ground and clutched wildly at the blackened earth.   He begged and pleaded with the fairy for mercy, but the fairy only shook his head.   Finally the farmer desperately offered to give twice as many fields for the fairies to dance upon.

'No!' the fairy replied coarsley.   'What is done is done and there can be no turning back on your fate now, only the King of Annwn himself can will such a curse to be lifted.'

The farmer broke into even harder tears and entreated the fairy for mercy so sorrowfully that eventually the fairy granted him a concession.

'I will speak to my lord and tell him of your repentance.   Meet me three days hence to hear your fate,' he answered, and then was gone.

The farmer slept so bad for those three nights that the whole of fairyland may well have been dancing in his bed with him.   On the third day he met the fairy at the same spot, his face the palest of white and his hands shaking like

47

a leaf in the wind as he waited to hear his fate.

'The curse cannot be reprieved,' the fairy said solemnly. 'The king's word cannot be taken back for he is no teller of falsehood.'

The farmer's heart sank down to his shoes, but the fairy continued: 'However, let it not be said that the Lord of Annwn is a man without mercy. Because of your repentance you are to be spared further punishment. He will honour his word but you must honour your word to let the fairies return to the land that you assumed was yours to control.'

The farmer's sigh was one of great relief, but the fairy continued, pointing his sword at him for the third time.

'The curse will cease for you, but your generations to come shall feel the vengeance after your death.' Then the man was gone.

The farmer was pleased with what the fairy had said, and kept his promise. He was kept awake by the fairies most nights for the rest of his life, but learned to live with it soon enough.

A few times after he had last seen the red man, the voice could still be heard booming its familiar warning through the darkness:

'Vengeance cometh!' but the farmer took little notice.

In the blackness of the night the farmer would sometimes worry about the fate he had prescribed to his descendants. In the light of day, however, he would forget and go about his business as usual, caring only that he and his family were safe. Such are the minds of men.

The generations passed, the farmhouse fell to ruin and another was built, oaks withered and decayed while saplings grew their branches high towards the heavens. Time passed on, as did the sons and sons of the farmer. As is the way of most bad news the curse was almost forgotten and life passed normally on the farm of Pantannas.

Rhydderch, a young distant relative of the farmer was about to be married. He had fallen in love with Gwerfyl, a beautiful girl who lived at a farmhouse in the next valley called Pen Craig Daf. He had been betrothed to her since the summer and spent a lot of his time walking the hills late in the evenings to see his love for a few precious hours. Their families were committed to the union, both seeing how deep their love was for each other and how they both seemed to light up at the mere thought of one another.

At this time winter was upon them. It not being a time for pleasant days and gatherings, they vowed to be married as soon as the first flower broke through the cold earth. They promised that as the flower showed its beauty to the world so would they show their love for each other.

It was soon Christmas Day and the girl came to Rhydderch's house for a fine meal of roast goose and winter vegetables. The day passed quickly for them together and by the time night had fallen both lovers were huddled together by the fire. Tales were told of humour, valour and adventure, and the whole company indulged in the merriment of the special occasion.

The laughter was silenced in an instant by a cry that

49

came from the river.

'The time for revenge has come!'

Everybody looked about in fright, chilled by the un-earthly sound. A few brave souls ventured out to see if they could hear anything further but all they could hear was the cascading of the river in flood. Soon enough though the voice could be heard again, louder still.

'The time has come!'

The house was deathly quiet; no one spoke, so great was their fright. Then screams pierced the night again as the house shook so hard that the doors rattled in their frames and bowls and plates fell crashing from the table on to the floor. All huddled to the floor, covering their heads and fearing that the whole house would fall around their ears.

The shaking was replaced by a cackling from an old woman standing at the doorway. Where she had come from nobody knew nor particularly wanted to know as the old crone started to cackle a hideous cackling laughter.

'Where are you from?' asked Rhydderch's father nervously, it being common courtesy to inquire as to a stranger's birthplace and destination.

'From Gerwyn Fach, Gerwyn Fawr and Gerwyn Ganol, the Three Pools of Blight!' answered the old witch, referring to the three pools on the river beneath the waterfalls where many a villager had drowned in times of flood.

'What do you want here, ugly hag?' one of the geusts had the courage to inquire.

'I want nothing that you could give me boy!' she spat. 'I came to give you warning of the fate that was to befall two families in this room, a thing that will not come lightly but that will bring pain and heartache to all of you here. You all have learnt nothing about my people and as you treat me with insults and contempt you shall remain ignorant.'

'If it concerns us, tell us please; we meant you no injury.' said Rhydderch's father.

'Your regret once again comes too late, I will tell you nothing except that a woman's heart shall seek till death but all she will find will be emptiness and pain until she breathes her last.' And with that the witch disappeared as quickly as she had arrived, leaving the guests looking bemused.

'The time for vengeance has come!' The cry sounded from the river for a third time, then all was silent.

After that the merriment ended for good. Although people tried to regain their joviality, their hearts had been dulled with dread from the witch's cold words.

The other guests left, being careful to avoid the river on their way home, and Rhydderch left to escort Gwerfyl home to Pen Craig Daf through the dark night.

On the way they held each other close under the stars, not wishing to part for the night. They promised each other their undying love, and after the witch's dreadful tidings promised to each other that even if death should intervene and take one of them away, their love would remain strong.

Just before Rhydderch left to travel back home to

51

Pantannas, he gave Gwerfyl a light kiss.

'I'll love you forever,' Gwerfyl said.

'And I you,' Rhydderch replied, and he left into the night full of the joys of youth.

By the morning he hadn't returned to Pantannas. His family became panic stricken and set out to Pen Craig Daf to find him. Gwerfyl had not seen him since the night before either. They feared the worse and searched high and low for Rhydderch; they looked on every hill top, under every tree and along evey stretch of the river. They even searched the three pools that the witch had said were her home, but he was nowhere to be found, neither was any trace of him uncovered. Gwerfyl waited for the fairies to appear that night to entreat them for news, but they were not to be seen that night, nor on any night after that.

Grief filled Gwerfyl and Rhydderch's parents. Knowing that the fairy folk were involved in his disappearance they went to Gweiryd, a sorcerer who lived as a hermit in a cave further up in the mountains. They told him the whole story about the voice from the river, the witch's warning, and the man's disappearance, and asked if there were any way that he could find Rhydderch or tell them anything of his fate.

The old man replied that the witch's warning about revenge must have fallen on Rhydderch. 'I know of a faded memory of a curse being taken by the fairies at Pantannas, though I know not why it has fallen on you. Rhydderch has been taken by the *Tylwyth Teg*. He is in a safe place and he will return, but time in the Otherworld runs differently to

ours and you will not see him alive again, unless some good chance befalls you.' Gwerfyl's heart sank and she began to weep with a sorrow deeper than any ocean.

Time passed and Rhydderch's mother and father lived in sadness until their graves took them. People came and went in the farmhouse of Pantannas and memories of Rhydderch's disappearance were soon forgotten. Some ignorant fools merely dismissed the story saying that he had merely run away from Gwerfyl, 'and who would blame him,' they would say after the sad and lonely woman had walked past.

Gwerfyl did not forget the curse so easily and was seen every day at Pantannas. Before the sun had risen in the west she could be seen standing atop the highest point on the farm, sometimes gazing into space but mostly searching the land around for any sign of her lover. She would stand there all day wrapped in her heavy cloak through rain, snow, fog or wind until the sun sank into the far-off land and darkness came.

Years passed of this and her beauty vanished to be replaced by a weathered and saddened face full of yearning and anguish. White streaks topped her deep brown hair, wrinkles spread across her once smiling face and her eyes grew weak through overuse.

One night she did not return from the lonely hilltop and in the morning she was found cold dead, her eyes still gazing over the empty land that had denied her happiness. She was buried in a chapel on the other side of The Fan, the

53

hill that she had spent so much of her life upon.

Years passed as did the memory of Rhydderch's and Gwerfyl's fate. The farm of Pantannas went through many families who either moved on or died out. The fairies were still quiet in Pantannas and most people thought that not too bad a thing.

As to what happened to Rhydderch that night, he actually came to no harm. His heart had been heavy with the events of the night but as he walked home he was uplifted by his love for Gwerfyl. By chance or fate his route took him through the fields. At that time they were thick with the dark green fairy rings that had once been ploughed over by a relative he had never even met.

As he stepped through one of the rings he heard a sweet sound coming from afar. It was the sweetest harp tune he had ever heard, and further away he could hear a soft gentle voice singing a beautiful song of love. So enchanted was he by this music that he forgot all sense and walked towards the sound. It led him to the Raven's Rift and to the mouth of a small cave in the hillside.

The singing was drifting out of the cave mouth, so he entered and sat down, entranced by the exquisite song from the Otherworld. A day passed but no hunger gripped him, and he longed only to hear the singing. After a few days his senses returned and he realised that everyone would be worrying about him. He asked of the angelic voice whether he could leave.

The voice drifted away into silence and he left the cave

to be greeted by the brightest of sunshine and the clearest of blue skies. Looking up at the sky and the bright flowers of summer on the hill top he became very puzzled. He walked towards Gwerfyl's house, eager to see his love on such a strangely beautiful winter's day. Rounding The Fan he was astonished to see that the chapel itself had disappeared and only plain ground remained.

Realising something was very wrong he ran all the way to Pen Craig Daf. When he arrived there he found only strangers who looked at him as if he were mad when he asked of a girl called Gwerfyl. He ran even quicker to Pantannas, noticing on the way that where forests of oak trees had once proudly stood were now just grassy fields.

The farm at Pantannas had also changed as he knocked on the strange door. An old man answered and seeing the frightened look on the breathless young man invited him in immediately. He offered Rhydderch a seat but the man just gazed in disbelief at the foreign interior of what had only days before been his own home.

Rhydderch asked where his father had gone and why the old man was living in his house. The old man looked at him strangely, then asked the young man's name.

'I am Rhydderch,' he replied, and the old man went pale.

'I have heard tell of you from my grandfather. I only thought it a tale! You have been gone for hundreds of years young man!'

Rhydderch sat down in a heap on a chair and gazed at the floor in despair. The old man, seeing his suffering, placed a hand on Rhydderch's shoulder to comfort him, but he just crumbled into dust.

The old man told this tale to others but was met with disbelief when he told them that the heap of dust had only hours before been a young man. The old man however could not bring himself to throw the ashes away like plain rubbish. He took them up The Fan and buried them on the site of the old chapel where he remembered praying as a boy.

Gwerfyl had been in the Otherworld listening to the sweet music of the fairies for what seemed like only a few days when Rhydderch walked over the hill to greet her. They remain together to this day."

Stories such as these are numerous in the folklore of all the Celtic-speaking countries. Usually the people live in the Otherworld for what seems like a few days or months only to return and find that 'real' time has flown by. The realisation that everyone you love is dead and buried and all are strangers must be one of the worst things the storytellers thought could happen.

Other stories tell of people being enticed into fairy rings where they end up dancing wildly with the energetic fairies. Their friend or partner, on the advice of a local wise man or woman, usually only manages to pull them out after a whole year has passed. When released they are completely exhausted and complain that they wanted to continue to dance, not realising quite how fast time flies when you are having fun!

The land of the fairies proves irresistible in the Irish myth of the *Voyage of Bran* dating from the eleventh century. Bran hears beautiful fairy music while asleep and when he wakes finds a blossoming silver branch lying next to him. A fairy woman appears singing of the glories of an island where she lives with thousands of other women, praising its music, wonderful trees and lack of death. The silver branch, a symbol of the Otherworld, leaps into her hand before she disappears back to her homeland.

Bran is determined to find this island, so he sets out to sea with his comrades. They travel through many magical islands and encounter dragons, giants, and other strange beasts until finding the Island of Women. While there they eat and drink the fine foods and ale of the Otherworld and also take the fairy women for wives, the time they spend there seeming to pass in a dream.

They soon get homesick however and long to see Ireland again, if only for a short time. The women warn them not to set foot on soil, but when they reach the coast one of the men leaps out and, like Rhydderch, immediately turns into ashes. Bran has to relate his adventures while in the boat, and then he disappears for ever.

The land of the fairies, although containing plenty of delicious food and being free from pain, is obviously not meant to be a place that mortals can merely visit. The price of otherworldly pleasures is high indeed, which is why an invitation from the fairies, however attractive, should never be taken up lightly!

THE LOST CHILD
OF LLANFABON

Not far from the setting of the last story is the parish of Llanfabon. It is a tiny village on the eastern border of Mid Glamorgan and contains a church dedicated to St Mabon. There are many Mabons in the myth and legends of the Welsh though quite which one the church is dedicated to is uncertain.

In the Mabinogion Mabon is a divine god of light, similar in many ways to Christ. The church may have been dedicated to a later Christianised version of this Mabon. In the same way churches named after Saint Bride in Ireland and Scotland are dedicated to a modified version of the Celtic goddess Brighid, or Brigit. This may seem like a strange concept but when Christianity first came to Britain and Ireland it merged quite peacefully with the older religion of the Celts. Many of the druids and chieftains accepted the belief in Jesus because it did not conflict with the belief in the divine child Mabon.

58

This tale also comes from the memory of Mr Craigfryn Hughes. The whole area around Quaker's Yard and Llanfabon seems to have teemed with the fairy folk. Nearby is a place called Pant y Dawns which means 'Dance Hollow,' referring of course to the dances of the *Tylwyth Teg*. The story serves as a sure warning not to leave any children unattended near where the fairy rings grow:—

"In a farmhouse called Berth Gron lived a young widow. Her only comfort in the dark years after the loss of her husband was her young child Griff. He was a strong and healthy child who liked nothing more than to play by himself in the green fields of the parish of Llanfabon. His mother was not too keen on the young one's wandering habits after the untimely death of her lover and sought to protect him from danger. She kept a tight reign on the child and would not let him out of her sight for even a moment.

It was not just the fear of some misfortune affecting the child that caused her to be so protective. The fairies of Llanfabon were large in number and fairy rings covered the fields as far as the eye could see. These fairies danced and sang songs as all fairies do but were different in one respect; they were incredibly ugly.

Their ugliness was almost matched by their love of tricking the unfortunate inhabitants of Llanfabon. Many times had unsuspecting people been lured into the fairy rings on a full moon never to be seen again. They also used sweet music to entice the farmers while they returned home from the fields. The farmers were only released from this magic spell when they found themselves stuck fast in one of the local bogs. The fairies of Llanfabon were a thorn in the side of the local people but as no one knew how to get rid of them without incurring their anger they had to put up with them. It is understandable then why the widow did not want to let her precious son out of her sight for even a moment. The fairies must have found Griff and his mother quite an irresistible challenge.

One windy morning just after dawn the widow was in the kitchen when she heard a loud braying coming from the cows. The milk from the cows was her only means of living and she couldn't chance anything unfortunate happening to them. After checking on Griff, who lay asleep in his cot she ran out of the house to the cow shed.

As soon as she got there the cows fell silent, though she was quite certain she could hear a tiny laughter on the breeze. She quickly dashed back into the house only to find that Griff's cot lay empty.

Her panic was tremendous as she frantically searched the house from top to bottom. There was no trace of him to be found and she ran to her neighbours who scoured the lands around looking for Griff but the child had simply disappeared. When sunset began to fall she sat alone in the house and started to cry tears of utter despair when she heard a voice from outside.

'Mummy,' the tiny voice said. She ran outside to see a small boy standing in front of her. The figure looked like her son and sounded like her son but her instincts told her that something was wrong.

'You are not my son!' she accused.

'I am.' the child said and walked towards her. The mother could do nothing but hug the child. Part of her thought that the child was not Griff but another part explained her doubts away. Maybe she was just being too suspicious, children of that age, especially healthy ones like Griff, grew and changed with every day that passed.

Days and months went by and sometimes the widow was glad to have her son back and other times she considered the boy a complete stranger. After a year had passed she knew that the small thing living in her house was definitely not her son.

Whereas Griff had been a strong and healthy young boy the thing in its place had not grown an inch in twelve months. Griff had also been a handsome boy and all the people of the village used to comment on how he had inherited his fathers charming looks. The thing living in the widows house had got uglier day by day and looked more like a wrinkled old man as time went by.

One day she'd had enough of telling herself that the thing was really Griff and, leaving the boy alone in the house, went to search for a way of getting rid of the ugly little creature.

Nearby in a castle called Castell y Nos, or Castle of the Night lived a wise man. The castle had been deserted for a long while because it was haunted by all manner of restless souls, the reason for this being that parts of the castle were built with stone from Llanfabon church.

The old man lived in a small wing of the castle. There had been a sorcerer or witch living there for as long as anyone could remember. Although some people said he was in league with the devil, most of the people of the district came to him for help when they had unusual troubles. He was well versed in fairy lore and the widow thought that he would be the one to know what to do about her son.

The old man greeted her cordially and she told him all about her son's disappearance and how something else had come back claiming to be her son.

'What does the child look like now?' asked the wise man

'Like a sour-faced and wrinkled old man,' she answered, and the wise man nodded his head.

'You must follow my instructions to be sure of what we are dealing with', he said. 'At noon tomorrow you must take the child into the kitchen and put him somewhere he can see you. Then you must take an egg and slice it down the middle. Throw one half away but with the other half take a spoon and whisk the egg in it round and round until it is beaten. You must make sure that the child is watching you while you are doing this but you cannot force him to watch or it will be spoiled.'

The widow was rather puzzled by these strange instructions but continued to listen to the old man.

'The child will ask you what you are doing when he sees you doing this and you must answer, "mixing the pastry for the reaper's pie". Then you must come to me and tell me his reply'.

Returning home the woman waited until the next day then did as she was advised. She sat the child on the floor and, cutting the egg in half, began to whisk the egg in its shell. The child was watching her doing this strange thing and sure enough asked her what she was doing.

'Mixing the pastry for the reaper's pies,' she replied.

'I have seen the acorn grow into an oak and I have seen the egg before the chicken but I have never heard of mixing pastry in an egg shell,' the child said angrily, looking even uglier and more wrinkled than before.

The widow went quickly to the castle and told the man what the child had said.

'It is certain then. The thing living with you is one of the old breed of fairies,' the man said. 'If you want to see your child again you must go to the crossroads on the road above Rhyd y Gloch. The full moon will appear in four days time and that is the night that you must go. Hide yourself very carefully in the bushes but keep an eye on all of the roads. Whatever you see on the crossroads you must keep yourself hidden and stay calm. If you betray yourself everything will be lost and you are likely never to see your son again.'

Again the widow was puzzled by these instructions but she trusted the old man's wisdom. When the full moon came about she wrapped up in her cloak and went to the crossroads, hiding herself carefully where she could see all of the four roads.

The night was cold and dead silent. After waiting for a couple of hours she began to doubt what the old man had said but she had no other choice but to wait.

After another hour or so the silence of the night was gently broken by the sound of music from afar. The widow watched the road carefully and felt a chill in her spine as the music got closer and closer.   Soon enough she saw a group of small figures approaching the crossroads. They were tiny people, the tallest of them was only waist height, and they were prancing along the road dancing and singing merrily in the moonlight.

She thought her eyes were deceiving her when she saw in the midst of the group her son Griff. He was dancing as happily as the rest of the procession and hadn't changed a bit since she last saw him. Her heart leaped and she was about to run out and grab her son back when she remembered the wise man's words.

It took great strength for her to stay hidden when her beloved son was only yards from her but she remained in the bushes until the fairies had passed. She waited a moment longer, then walked home, happy at seeing Griff alive after so long but not able to stop the tears rolling down her cheeks.

When she returned home she did not want to face the ugly thing living in her house, especially as it called her mum. She decided however that it was in the best interests of her real son if she acted normally to the ugly child, so she treated it with the same love and tenderness that she had showed Griff.

Returning to the magician she explained all that she saw at the crossroads that night. The old man took out a big black book and poured over it murmuring to himself as he did so. After a while he shut the book with a quick snap and told the widow what to do next.

'You must find a pure black hen with not a single white feather upon it nor any other that is not of the deepest

The Fairy Exchange

black. Then you must bake it in front of a wood fire, feathers and all else intact until the house starts to fill up with smoke. Shut all the doors and windows and block up any holes in the house except one. Do not look at the ugly child, only watch the hen and when all of its feathers have dropped of then you can look around.'

The old man wished her good luck and after thanking him for all his help the widow left to find the hen. She searched for hours, visiting every farmhouse that she could walk to but she could not find a pure black hen. A white or grey feather always managed to appear somewhere on the birds. Night was falling and she got to the point of despair when all of a sudden a black hen strode out from under a hedgerow, as black as the darkest of nights.

Quickly gathering it up she ran home as quick as she could. The ugly child was crying and moaning at her for leaving it alone all day but she ignored its whines and put the hen on the fire. When all the doors and windows were blocked, apart from a small gap high up on the wall, she sat facing the fire and waited. She said more prayers in that one night than she had in all her Sundays.

Soon enough the house began to fill up with thick white smoke and the child began to whine loader then ever before. As the smoke filed her nostrils she felt her head cloud up and she fainted.

Sweet music filled her ears when she first awoke and she recognised the music as the same she had heard at the crossroads. Looking at the hen she saw that all of its feathers had fallen to the floor and quickly peering through the smoke she saw that the ugly baby was gone.

'Mummy!' a little voice called from outside.
She jumped up and ran outside. Her little Griff was standing there looking a little thin and bedraggled but smiling his sweet smile.

'Where on earth have you been?' she asked, lifting him up in her arms and hugging him tightly.

'I've been dancing mummy,' was all the child could say as his mother took him into the house".

This story is a good enough reason for children to listen to their parents when warned not to stay out at night! Such tales are widespread in the folklore of the Celtic countries and are even found in Scandinavia. Finding out that the child was really a fairy was the difficult part and involved a lot of trickery and riddles

In Breton legends there is a tale when a meal for ten workers is brewed in an eggshell to fool the fairies. Another precaution taken to ensure the baby was not kidnapped was to leave some iron in the shape of a poker, tongs or knife over it. It was well known that the fairies were unable to go anywhere near iron. The baby was usually only under threat if it had not been baptised and special vigilance was needed at St John's Eve when the fairies were meant to be particularly busy.

The description of the child looking as if it were old may relate to mental or physical disabilities and the fairy kidnapping story may have been made up to account for this. A thirty year old dwarf living at the start of this century in Brittany was called a Corrigan, a Breton word for fairy, by his own mother who also said that he was not the child she gave birth to.

The story may also have a more sinister background as a reason to get rid of poorly and sickly children in an age when health could mean survival for the whole family. The Norse practice of leaving the child alone on a mountain top for one night to see if it survived was for a similar reason.

The disappearance of children also occurs widely in the Celtic legends. In the Mabinogion tale of *Pwyll Prince of Dyfed*, Rhiannon, a horse goddess, has a child by Pwyll. On the night after its birth the women looking after it all fall asleep and wake to find the child gone. They panic, afraid that they will be blamed so they kill a deer's pup, smearing the blood and bones over the cot and the sleeping Rhiannon. When she wakes she is blamed for the child's death. Her punishment for this is to stand at the mounting block and carry all of the guests into the court of Arbeth on her back.

At this time the lord of Gwent Is-Coed, Teyrnon Twryf Liant, had a mare that foaled every May Eve. The colt always disappeared however and that night he resolved to watch the mare. Soon enough the mare foaled and a large claw came into a window and grabbed the new born foal. Teyrnon saved the mare then went out to give chase to the strange beast. When he returned he found a baby in the stable and reared it as his own until discovering that it is Pwyll's child. When it is handed back the child is named Pryderi, meaning 'care' or 'thought', after Rhiannon's anguish.

The baby's disappearance must have been due to the inhabitants of the Otherworld. The story survives in a mutated form however and it is hard to distinguish why the child is taken and to whom the mysterious claw belongs. The kidnapping of the baby must have had some importance to the plot at some time; possibly its real father was from the Otherworld, a common theme in birth tales of heroes like Pryderi.

With the baby-snatching theme it is easy to see a link between the royal tales surviving in the manuscripts and those lasting in the folklore of the common people. Another survival in this tale is the wise old man or sorcerer who appears in many folk tales. These wise men, witches, sorcerers, and magicians can be traced back to the old classes of druids, and later, bards in Wales.

Peter Berresford Ellis in his recent study of the druids cites an abundance of evidence that shows that the druids did not die out completely after the Roman Invasion. Instead they changed their position in society to reappear as the mystics and wise villagers of popular folklore. Such people were associated with the devil after the Christian period but they were probably just continuing the old practice of magic and fairy-lore.

The social position of these magicians was greatly reduced, hence their occupation of caves and abandoned castles, but the local people still obviously went to them for advice and held a lot of respect for them. A lot of their knowledge would have been lost since the far off days of the druids but they clearly still knew how to deal with the mischievous fairies.

THE LADY
OF THE LAKE

Lake legends are an important part of Celtic mythology. Everybody is familiar with the Lady of the Lake who gives Arthur his sword Excalibur. This lady comes from the parish of Ystrad Dyfodwg. A lake there is named Llyn y Forwyn, 'The Damsel's Pool'. It is also known as Llyn Nelferch, for a reason soon to be made clear, and lies half way between a farm house called Rhondda Fechan and the Vale of Safrwch. The tale is very similar to the more famous legend of Llyn y Fan in Carmarthenshire but is in no way inferior:—

"An unmarried farmer lived at a farmhouse called Rhondda Fechan or 'Little Rhondda.' He lived with his widowed mother and was quite sad that he had found nobody to share his life with. To try and ease the loneliness he would go for long walks around the hills and valleys. He found comfort in the soft contours of the land

and would try to imagine a beautiful girl walking alongside him.

Usually he would stop by the side of the nearby lake and gaze into the clear blue water. The ripples on the surface of the water made all sorts of shapes and he would attempt to discern some omen, imagining a face appearing here and a figure appearing there.

One day as he was sitting by the lake he actually did see a woman! She was walking along the opposite bank, dressed in a flowing deep blue robe that rippled in the gentle breeze blowing across the lake. Even though she was far off he could see how she walked with a light, graceful step. He quickly ran around the lake to talk to her.

As he got closer she turned around to face him, causing his greeting words to stick fast in his throat. Her face was of the purest white and the fairest he had ever seen in all his life. He didn't know what to do at all. Eventually he meekly offered her some of the bread he had brought for his lunch as a gift.

'Your bread is too hard for me!' she said, and dived into the water. The farmer was stunned and waited around to see if she would return but she did not. He vowed to come back at the same time the next day and bring some unleavened bread to see whether she would accept that.

Sure enough the next morning she was walking along the other side of the lake, he ran around and offered her the soft dough.

'Would you eat the bread you have offered me!' she replied in disgust, jumping swiftly back into the waters of the lake.

He returned home disheartened and told his mother what had happened. She knew a little about the fairies, for that is what the woman must have been, and advised him to take some half baked bread as a compromise.

So the next day he set out as before. He saw the fairy woman by the side of the lake as usual and chased after her offering her the bread. Much to his delight this time she took it from him and began to eat it.

'Hello,' she said, one small word that sounded so magical and soothing to his ears. The farmer was too stunned by the beauty and softness of her voice even to reply and just stared at her in a trance.

'Who are you?' the farmer eventually asked wide eyed once he regained his voice, rudely forgetting to return her greeting.

'I am Nelferch,' she replied in a soft voice that drifted across the air as a wave floats over a pool.

'Where are you from?' the farmer asked, again forgetting his manners and not telling the woman his name.

'I am from these waters', she answered, spreading her hand over the lake. 'I live there with my cattle at the bottom of the lake.'

The farmer was not too concerned that she was a fairy; he had heard of mortals living in worse places, and besides he felt a sudden deep love for the woman.

'Will you be my wife?' the farmer asked, not able to control the strong feelings he already had for the fairy woman.

'Why we have only just met!' she smiled.

The farmer pleaded with the woman for most of the

71

day but she only answered in riddles or declined politely. Soon enough however he could see in her smile and in her eyes the same affection that he held for her. The farmer continued to plead with her, promising her almost the world for her hand, until she eventually agreed as is the strange way with love.

'I will marry you on the one condition,' the fairy woman said, 'that we shall not disagree. To argue is to bring disharmony and if we dispute each other three times I shall leave you and return to the lake, taking all my possessions with me.

The farmer could only nod his head and gaze into the deep blue waters of her eyes.

They were married within days and Nelferch brought her cattle from the lake to the surface. There was plenty of them and they were the healthiest cattle that anyone had ever seen. Once they were brought onto the farm they produced an abundance of milk. From then on the farm grew and prospered like none other in the region.

The maiden and the farmer also lived together in great comfort and happiness for many years. This time the farmer used to walk up to the lake hardly believing that the lady of his dreams was actually by his side. No man could have been happier than he.

One day one of their neighbours died. He had been an old man and had lived a long full life. The last few years of his life had been full of suffering, so everyone was relieved that his pain had finally passed.

Nelferch flew into a rage of tears at the funeral. She lamented and cried uncontrollably, screaming and tearing at her hair. Nobody else, not even the relatives of the man were behaving like this and the farmer chided Nelferch, telling her to be quiet.

'Why do you grieve so hard when his suffering is finally over?' he asked her.

'I grieve for that mans life in the next world,' she answered. 'It will be full of eternal misery and torment for the pain that he caused so many in this life, and you have also made the first disagreement'.

The next few months went by as happy and as peaceful as ever and he forgot about the funeral. Soon enough Nelferch had a child, a beautiful baby boy and the farmer was even happier than he had been before.

When the child died he was inconsolable and stricken with grief. Nelferch could only laugh and sing around the house and this angered him greatly.

'Why do you laugh at the death of your child? Do your kind not love your own children?' he asked bitterly.

'I loved that child as much as you did, which is why I laugh,' she answered. 'He has left this wicked world and gone to the Otherworld where all he will know will be happiness and eternal life, something you have yet to discover. You have also now made the second disagreement'.

The next few months were hard but the time he shared with the woman he loved soon made up for the loss of his son. The farm continued to prosper and the cows grew in number so much that the farmer's land was to small to contain all of them. His widowed mother was very poor and lived nearby at Ty Fry, the House up the Hill, so he took a few of the cows and gave them to her.

When Nelferch found out she flew into a rage and ordered him to take the cattle back immediately.

'Why should I take them back when we have such plenty and she has nothing?' he asked.

'I do not disagree with your charity but you gave them to her without asking me. The cows belong to me even though we are married. In giving them away you have showed that you think you own me as well as my property. I remain a free person. We have now disagreed three times and I am gone.'

With that she gathered up all of her cows, calling the ones from Ty Fry with a gentle song. No amount of pleading on the part of the farmer could stop her as she walked away to the lake with the cows following in a trail behind her. As they reached the lake they sank quickly back into their home, leaving the farmer alone once more on the banks. His heart sank deeper than any water and he returned to the lake as much as he could, longing to see even just a glimpse of Nelferch. She never reappeared but the farmer often heard the sound of her singing being carried on the wind. When he heard this sad remnant of what he had lost tears rolled from his cheeks, adding to the quiet waters of the lake".

Lakes were a source of great power to the Celts and were home to gods and goddesses as well as fairies. Offerings were made in abundance to bodies of water such as lakes and rivers. A lake in Anglesey, called Llyn Cerrig Bach, was found full of a large hoard of metal objects that

74

had been deposited as offerings.

The Romans as they invaded Gaul in the first century BC found lakes that were full of gold and precious metals. So much treasure had been deposited in some lakes that the Greek writer Posidonius tells us that they were even sold off by auction.

The legend of Llyn y Fan is almost identical to the Llyn y Nelferch story. Here a man sees the lady swimming in the lake and tries to entice her to the shore with bread. As with the story just told it is only when he half bakes the bread that she accepts it.

She likes the man but her father comes with her two identical sisters and says that he will only give her away if he can recognise which one she is. He is very hard pressed to tell them apart for they are perfectly alike but one woman gently points her foot out. He sees from the way her shoe is tied differently that she is the one. Luckily for him he had earlier been admiring the beauty of her ankles.

She agrees to marry him but on the condition that he does not strike her three times. Her father gives her a gift of as many animals as she can count in one breath and they bring great prosperity to the couple. As usual the happiness does not last long. The first blow occurs when she will not go to a christening and he jokingly taps her with a glove to get her moving. The second occurs at a wedding when she bursts into tears and he places a hand on her shoulder while asking what is wrong. The third and final blow comes when she laughs at a funeral, happy for the person's transition to the Otherworld. He places a hand on her to stop her from laughing and she leaves taking her magical

75

cattle with her.

In the Irish legends of the warband the Fianna an ugly woman comes to the house where they are gathered and asks for entry. None of the men want her to enter because of her repulsive features apart from Diarmaid. He is polite to the woman and invites her in, being so courteous that he even invites her to share his bed for the night. When they go to sleep she transforms into a beautiful woman. They fall in love and she builds a large castle for him on Ben Endain hill, agreeing to live with him only on the condition that he does not upbraid her three times. Obviously he breaks this rule and she vanishes, taking the castle with her.

Although fairy women have great beauty and riches we can see that when they live with mortals they are incompatible. The magical triple condition that must not be broken is always unavoidably fulfilled. The lake fairies are made out to have greater wisdom and understanding than the mortals and the union of fairy and human ends in disaster.

These tales are all that remain in Glamorgan of what must have once been a wealth of material concerning lakes. These features of the landscape had their own spirits and they were venerated in the same way as holy wells or hills, usually for their healing powers.

When Christianity came to Europe statues of the Virgin Mary or saints were laid on the shores of lakes and rivers to convert their use from paganism to Christianity. The fairies in the Welsh lake legends are probably the last remnants of these spirits or goddesses of the waters.

76

THE SPARROWHAWK
KNIGHT

The Celtic legends of Wales were easily influenced in the middle ages by the age of chivalry. The legends changed and the old Celtic gods and goddesses were transplanted into the romantic world of the Norman-French knights. The tales are set in a more realistic, less magical world but they are still very powerful, and abound with the wonder that is the age of King Arthur.

The Mabinogion has a number of these chivalrous romances within it. Part of this tale occurs in Cardiff, or Caerdyf, and is found in *Gereint Son of Erbin*. The background to this episode must be explained first as the story is a long one.

Arthur's wife, Gwenhwyfar, has been accidentally left behind while Arthur and his retinue are out hunting for a large majestic stag. She follows the trail of the hunt with one of her maidens and along the way they meet Gereint, a knight of Arthur's court. As they continue following the hunt they meet a dwarf, a lady and an unknown heavily armoured knight on a large charger.

Gwenhwyfar sends her maiden to ask the knight's name but the dwarf refuses to answer her and strikes the maiden across the face. Gereint is angered by this and also goes to the dwarf to ask the knight's name but he too is struck by the dwarf. He is about to kill the dwarf but realises that without his armour he is no match for the mysterious knight.

This sets the plot for the rest of the story as he vows to avenge the insult that Gwenhwyfar's maiden and he himself suffered. Following the group as they leave, Gereint promises to send news to Gwenhwyfar the next evening:—

"They travelled past Caerleon and across a ford on the river Usk, travelling across flat fertile plains until they reached a walled town. The knight and lady that Gereint followed were greeted by a great crowd of people who came from every house in the town to cheer them.

Gereint found that the town was called Caerdyf and looked in the houses to see if he could find anyone he knew to loan arms from. All the people he found were strangers but there were plenty of arms and armour. In all the houses men were preparing their shields and armour, sharpening their swords and shodding their horses in preparation for some great event.

The dwarf, lady and knight went into a castle at the centre of the town. They were greeted from the battlements and streets by throngs of people and Gereint waited to see if they would stay at the castle.

When they did not emerge from the castle Gereint went off to search for lodgings. Most of the inns were full of armed men and their retinues but he spotted an old ruined court and a broken down hall a little way out of the town. He headed there to make himself known to the owner.

The court was deserted and ruined apart from a marble staircase on which sat an old man dressed in rags. Gereint examined the old man.

'What are your thoughts knight?' the man asked.

'I wonder where I shall stay tonight for I know nobody here,' Gereint answered

'You may stay here if you wish,' the old man said, gesturing at the ruined court with his arm. 'I will provide for you the best I can.'

'I will stay.' Gereint said, 'and I thank you for your offer, what is your name?'

'I am Ynywl, and you?'

'Gereint son of Erbin.

He dismounted from his horse and followed the old man up the stairs to a chamber. In the chamber sat an old woman dressed in tattered silk clothes. Gereint saw that when new the clothes would have been fit for a queen and when young the woman would have been fairer than any maiden he had ever seen.

Sitting across from her was a young girl dressed in old dowdy clothes. She was more beautiful and graceful than anyone at Arthur's court apart from Gwenhwyfar herself. Gereint felt that he had fallen in love with her already. Ynywl asked her to attend to the knight and the horse and

she did so better than any groom. She was then sent out to
the town to acquire some food and soon enough returned
with some mead, meat and bread.

'These were the best that I could buy,' she told her
father, looking ashamed that she was unable to buy more.

The meat was cooked and they sat down to their meal,
Gereint sitting between the old man and his wife and the
young girl serving them. After they finished the meal the
two men started to talk.

'Was it you who built this court?' Gereint asked.

'It was I indeed who built and owned not only this
court but also the castle and town that you have just ridden
through,' he answered.

'How did you lose it?' inquired Gereint.

'I will tell you the tale for I was known as earl Ynywl
and lost a great amount of land. My nephew, my brother's
son, took control of his father's domains after his death
while still a young boy. I took them into my own and ruled
over them until the boy became a man. I foolishly kept his
lands from him and he waged war against me, overcoming
me and taking all that I had from me. That is why I now
live here in these ruins.'

'Who was the knight with the lady and dwarf that I
followed to the castle and why is there such a preparation
to arms in the town?' asked Gereint, eager to learn all that
he could about the stranger.

'The preparation is for a great contest that is to take
place tomorrow outside the town. The young earl will take
a forked stick and plant it in the ground. Upon that stick he
will place a silver rod and upon that rod the greatest

sparrowhawk you will ever see. Everyone in the town will go there with the woman they love the best for no one can joust for the sparrowhawk unless they have a love with them.'

'What of the knight then?' Gereint asked.

'The knight that you saw has won the sparrowhawk twice already. The lady was his lover and the dwarf his attendant. If he wins the contest this year he will keep the sparrowhawk for ever and will be named Knight of the Sparrowhawk.'

'I must ask you for advice,' Gereint said, 'for I wish to fight the knight for an insult his dwarf caused myself and one of the fair Gwenhwyfar's maidens.' Then Gereint related the tale of the insult to Ynywl.

'My council is that it is not easy for you to fight tomorrow for you come here alone and unprepared. I will loan you my own arms and my horse if you wish but you have no love for whom to fight for the sparrowhawk,' Ynywl said.

'My own horse I will keep but I will loan your arms and if it pleases you I will fight for your daughter in the contest. If I return from the fight I will take her to be my love and my wife. If I die and do not return I promise that she will come back to you untouched by my hand'.

'My daughter Enid will go with my blessing but you must be ready with horse and arms tomorrow. When the knight's lady goes to take the sparrowhawk you must be ready to oppose it. We will accompany you and I will act as your squire,' Ynywl said.

That evening they prepared for the next day and retired

to sleep early. Before dawn they rose and dressed and Gereint made ready his horse and arms. By the time dawn came they were all stood on the meadow listening to the proclamation of the unknown knight.

'Take the sparrowhawk my lady', said the knight to his lady. Last year it was yours and the year before that. This year I shall defend it for you for all the years to come. If there is anyone here who tries to deny you the bird I will defend it.'

'Do not take it lady', shouted Gereint, mounting his horse and moving forward through the crowd. 'This year it does not belong to you for there is a maiden here more comely and beautiful than thee and of more noble a birth, it is she who shall take it'.

The challenge was set and the knight mounted his own horse and they moved closer together, Gereint and his horse both standing proud in their rusted heavy armour.

They charged each other fiercely and both their spears broke on the others' shields under the force of their assault. New spears were brought to them and they were also broken, and the next and the next after that. The old man bringing Gereint his weapons and the dwarf bringing the knights.

When the next spear broke Ynywl went up to Gereint and handed him a magnificent well crafted spear.

'This is the spear that was given to me when I became a knight, it has never broken or bent in all the years I have used it,' he said as Gereint gratefully took the spear. Likewise the dwarf went up to the night and handed him a terrible long biting spear.

'Remember my lord that this is the spear that has defeated many a proud enemy and you have never lost whilst it was in your grip,' said the dwarf.

Then they charged at each other a final time with a terrible hard fury and Gereint struck the knight's shield so that his spear passed through the centre of it, splitting it in two and piercing his armour. The force of the blow also broke his saddle straps and sent the knight over the back of his horse.

Gereint dismounted and withdrew his spear full of venomous anger. He charged at the knight who drew his spear and met his charge. They thrust and hacked at each other until both of their armour was broken and dented and blood and sweat covered their bodies.

The knight gave Gereint a powerful blow that pierced his armour and sorely wounded him. As he fell to the floor the old man rushed over to his side.

'Lord why do you fall in defeat when it was his dwarf that so badly insulted Gwenhwyfar's maiden and yourself?' Ynywl scolded. 'Where is your bravery and pride now?'

With that Gereint found the strength to bring himself and his sword up. With a new found strength he struck the knight on the head so that his helmet split and his skin and bone were sliced apart by the force of the blow. The knight fell defeated to the ground.

'I entreat thee for mercy,' the knight begged. 'A false pride and arrogance has made me ask this too late. If I do not have time to atone for my sins with a priest I will soon have no need to ask you for anything'.

'I will give you quarter,' Gereint replied, 'but you must

go and seek Gwenhwyfar at Arthur's court to make amends for the injury you have given to her maiden. You have now paid enough for the insult your dwarf gave to me but you must not dismount or stop to rest until you have been forgiven by Gwenhwyfar'.

'I will agree to your demands and though I may not make it that far I will go,' the knight replied. 'But before I go I must ask your name.'

'Gereint son of Erbin,' Gereint answered, 'and what is yours?'

'Edern son of Nudd.'

Then Gereint put the wounded knight on his horse and he went off towards Arthur's court with the lady, the dwarf and plenty of sorrow along with them.

The young earl of Caerdyf came to Gereint and gave the sparrowhawk to Enid. He introduced himself and his retinue and gave greetings to Gereint.

'Will you stay with me in celebration tonight?' the earl asked Gereint; 'for you have won the contest with great bravery.'

'No, I will stay tonight where I stayed last night,' Gereint answered.

'Then if you are not in my house you shall still receive my hospitality, I will send an abundance of whatever you require. I will ask my physicians to prepare a bath to heal you and ease your weariness,' the earl declared.

'I thank you,' Gereint said, and he left with Ynywl towards the ruined court.

When they arrived the earl's retinue were already there preparing a great feast in the hall. They made ready all of

84

the living quarters and filled the stores with meat, ale and bread.

A bath was made for Gereint and his wounds were covered with healing herbs and bandages. When he came into the hall the young earl and his wife and daughters were there ready to receive him.

'Where is Ynywl and his daughter?' Gereint asked.

'Ynywl and his wife are upstairs dressing their daughter in the fine clothes brought by me ready for the feast,' the earl answered.

'Let her remain in the clothes she is in now,' said Gereint; 'for it is only by Gwenhwyfar that I will allow her to be dressed with the finest garments that Arthur's court can provide'.

'So it shall be,' said the earl.

Enid was brought forth in her old clothes and she still outshone the best dressed women in the room, so great was her beauty and grace. Gereint sat down to eat with the young earl and Ynywl sat on one side and Enid and her mother on the other. Everyone else then sat according to their status and they ate their fill of food and drink, the old hall filling up with merriment once more.

'Will you come and stay with me on the morrow?' asked the young earl of Gereint.

'I will not, for it is to Arthur's court that I shall travel next and I go to seek justice for Ynywl for he has suffered without his domain for long enough.'

'Ynywl has had no injustice done to him by me, it is by his own deeds that he lost his lands', the young earl stated.

'That may be', said Gereint, 'but he will have his

earldom back unless death take me.'

'I will gladly abide by what council you give me Gereint,' said the earl. 'I see you are an impartial and honourable man and I am eager to end the hostilities between us, for he is still my mother's brother'.

'My council,' Gereint stated, 'is that the lands that once belonged to the earl are given back and that all the vassals needing to pay homage to him will do so tonight. Nothing that is not rightfully his will be given nor will the dishonour that he has suffered until today be reprieved.'

This was done and Ynywl was made an earl again. His men gave him homage and the castle, the town and the rest of his earldom were returned to him.

'You have given me back my realm,' Ynywl said to Gereint; 'please accept my daughter's hand with my blessing'.

'I will gladly take her to Arthur and Gwenhwyfar,' said Gereint. 'There she will be dressed in the finest of clothes and she will become my wife.'

So in the morning they set out for Arthurs court."

The Welsh influence in the medieval romantic tale is very apparent. The names of Arthur's knights in the French tales are mainly altered versions of the original Welsh names; Cei becomes Kay for example. A good argument has also been put forward for Chretien de Troyes' famous Arthurian stories to derive from Welsh originals.

Many of the Arthurian figures in the Mabinogion tales have earlier origins, and Gereint is no exception. He appears as a historical figure in an ancient Welsh poem from the *Black Book of Carmarthen*, which dates from around the year 1200 AD. He is described as a resistance fighter from the dark ages and there must have existed heroic tales concerning his life and deeds. It was only later than he evolved into one of Arthur's medieval knights in the Mabinogion.

These romances in the Mabinogion tell us that King Arthur's court was established at Caerleon. The nearby town in this story is Caerdyf, the old name for Cardiff which means the 'Fort on the River Taff' rather than the modern form of the Welsh which has degenerated to Caerdydd, or 'Day Castle.'

The castle that Gereint travelled to was the medieval motte and bailey still surviving within the later walls of Cardiff Castle. This castle was first built in wood around 1093 AD on the site of the earlier Roman fort whose surviving walls would have added to its defences. The later stone castle was built in the late twelfth century and this would have been the home of the young earl and where Edern son of Nudd, the enemy in this story, spent the night before the contest.

It is easy while walking around the old bailey in the grounds of Cardiff Castle to slip back into this romantic world of maidens and knights in shining armour. It is also refreshing to know that this was where Welsh knights such as Gereint, Cei, and Bedwyr were said to have fought and jousted in the dream world of the Arthurian romances.

ELIDORUS
IN THE OTHERWORLD

This story introduces the Celtic Otherworld. Known in Welsh as Annwn it is an ethereal place separate from this world but co-existing alongside it. It is variously situated in hills, mountains, islands, or as in this tale underground. It always lies just outside the bounds of reality and human sight. You could also only be invited to the Otherworld or stumble on it by accident, it was impossible to enter there at will.

This tale of the Otherworld survives in the writings of Gerald of Wales, one of the best literary sources for life in the Welsh middle ages. He was born in 1146 at Manorbier castle in Pembrokeshire into one of the greatest royal houses in Welsh history, the house of Dinevor. His father was Norman de Barri whose castle still remains at the sea port of Barry and his mother was named Angharad. Angharad was the daughter of Gerald of Windsor by Princess Nesta, 'Helen of Wales'. She was daughter of

Rhys ap Tewdwr Mawr, the last independent prince of South Wales.

This background made him very proud to be a Welshman which is why he called himself Giraldus Cambrensis, 'Gerald of Wales'. His young life was filled of the great stories of his family's achievements in Welsh history. He was also an ardent supporter of an independent Welsh church separate from Rome. He became the archdeacon of Brecknock and toured Wales in 1188 with Archbishop Baldwin of Canterbury to raise soldiers for the Third Crusade. What he experienced he recorded in his 'Itinerary of Wales,' a valuable record of life in medieval Wales. His tour took him through Glamorganshire and at Neath Abbey, founded in 1112 by Richard de Grainville, he recorded the tale of Elidorus:—

"Elidorus was twelve years old and studying under the tutelage of the monks at Neath Abbey. He was a constant daydreamer and his laziness towards his work meant that he frequently received beatings at the hands of the monks.

One morning he knew that he would be due for such a beating. He had spent the whole of the previous evening watching the clouds floating past, trying to make shapes out of them in his mind. The work he was supposed to be doing had been long forgotten.

It was almost midday and he was meant to have arrived for lessons at dawn. With his head pointed up to the sky and his mind wondering he ambled along the road. When he heard someone running towards him he turned quickly and saw his teacher coming towards him with a large stick. As fast as he could he fled off the road, running through the forest until he came to the river. Finding a hole in the riverbank he hid in it and waited for the monk to pass.

Hours went by but so worried was Elidorus that he stayed hidden, not wanting to risk being found and receiving his punishment. Hunger tightly gripped his stomach but two days later he was still lying beneath the riverbank, so great was his fear of the priests. He drifted in and out of sleep and on the evening of the second day two men appeared before him.

They were small men, only half the size of an adult and he had to blink and rub his eyes before he believed in them. They spoke to him with soft gentle voices that sounded like the blowing of the breeze.

'Come with us Elidorus, unless you want to stay here,' they said.

'Where are you going?' Elidorus asked.

'To the land you think of in your dreams,' they replied.

Elidorus liked this land a lot and eagerly followed the two small men as they walked off through the forest. They followed a small path and Elidorus soon found himself walking underground through a tunnel. It was a strange journey but soon enough they emerged out of the darkness into a beautiful country.

They were standing on a hill and could see the land stretching out before them. Lush green plains spread as far as the eye could see with deep blue rivers running through them. Forests of tall trees lay in clumps about the land, the thickets around them teeming with wild animals whose pelts were all coloured red and white. Beautiful birdsong filled the air from high above and Elidorus stood spellbound. He thought the sight was wonderful, it was like the land he had left behind but much more beautiful.

One thing was different though, light was shining out over the land but there was no sun to be seen. The sky was covered with thin hazy clouds but the soft white brightness illuminating the land was nothing like the sun's light.

He stood watching the scene for hours and he could have stayed there forever but soon night came. Elidorus looked up to watch the stars, another pastime of his, and he hoped they would be even brighter than normal. To his dismay the sky was pitch black and not a single star or moon hung in the sky.

He was taken by the two men to see the king. Entering the court he was awed by the magnificence of the hall and the assembly gathered inside it. All the people were the same height as his companions but they were dressed in the brightest and most elegant of garments which glittered with large jewels and gold embroidery. They all rushed around the hall, singing merrily and preparing for a great feast.

The king greeted him and looked at him closely for a while. He seemed pleased with Elidorus and smiled, introducing him to his son who was the same age only smaller. The boy showed him around the court introducing everyone to Elidorus. All the people were only waist high but they were perfectly proportioned. Long hair cascaded down the mens' as well as the women's shoulders and framed their beautiful soft pale faces in a golden glow.

The boy invited Elidorus to eat with him and they ate a

luxuriant meal of milk, honey and saffron, no meat or fish even showed on the table. Elidorus stayed with them for a while as a guest of the king. He soon learnt that they were a kind and gentle people who took oaths with no one and also never lied. They saw dishonesty as hideous and chided the selfishness and ambition of Elidorus's people. They worshipped no gods and only loved truth which they saw as more powerful than any god.

Elidorus settled in quickly and became good friends with the king's son, playing with him most days. Sometimes he would go for walks through the beautiful land to meet more of the fairies, all of whom were the most jovial and friendly people he had ever met.

Soon enough however he began to miss the clouds and stars that gave him so much pleasure in his world. One day he asked the king whether he could return briefly to his world. The king was dismayed but as Elidorus was such a good friend to his son he gave him leave to go, making him promise to return as soon as possible.

He left the Otherworld and visited his mother, telling her not to worry about him. He told her tales about the fairyland as best he could to someone who had not seen so much beauty. He visited her a lot in the next few weeks, always having new stories to tell of the beauty and pleasure he had seen.

One day he was telling his mother of the plentiful amount of gold the fairies had and how he used to play with a golden ball almost as big as his head. Hearing this she entreated him to bring some of the gold for her. Elidorus did not want to at first but his mother worked so hard only to remain poor. He thought his friends would not mind if he took only a small amount of their bountiful riches.

The next day, after returning to the fairy land, he played with the king's son. They had the gold ball and would run all over the land with it throwing it to each other and competing to see who could roll it the farthest. When the king's son tired of the game he left the ball with Elidorus and went to have a midday sleep. Elidorus took the ball, thinking it would not be missed if he accidently lost it. He ran all the way to his mother's house, not wanting to be seen by any of the fairies.

He reached the doorway of his home but in his excitement he tripped on the door step, dropping the ball which rolled into the room where his mother was sitting. He ran after it but before he could reach it a fairy appeared and grabbed it. The fairy gave Elidorus a look of such utter betrayal and contempt that the image stayed in his mind forever. Then he left, taking the gold ball with him.

Elidorus ran after the fairy feeling stupid to have listened to his mother's greed. He wanted to explain his actions and tell his friends that he was truly sorry, but the fairy had already gone. He searched all day and night for the path that would take him to the Otherworld but to no avail.

He slept in the hole in the riverbank that night, dreaming that the fairies would come back to him but they did not. In the morning he woke feeling cold, miserable and very ashamed. For a whole year he searched the riverbank and the forest looking for the doorway back into paradise but it remained well and truly hidden. Eventually he had to be dragged back to his house by his friends and mother, weeping uncontrollably.

Many years later after lots of hard study he became a priest at the abbey and devoted himself to the work of God. He would relate his story to anyone who doubted the existence of the fairies and even told the tale to the Bishop of St Davids. Every time he reached the end of the story he would cry with such sadness at his loss that no one left disbelieving his tale. He could be heard on sunny days singing and calling in the fairy tongue and would often recite it at prayer. The language sounded similar to the tongue of the ancient Britons but his calls and prayers were never answered."

Elidorus's sadness at losing the Otherworld for ever after tasting its delights is easily understood. It is a heavenly place of extreme beauty and prosperity. In the Otherworld a timeless immortality exists and the people who live there, the fairies, are the shrunken remnants of the old gods of the Celtic peoples. The Otherworld appears as the place where magic enters this world and where mortals travel to seek unlimited adventure.

In the Mabinogion tale of Pwyll Prince of Dyfed, Pwyll, while out hunting, meets Arawn the king of Annwn. Arawn has a problem with an enemy in the Otherworld and asks Pwyll to help him. They agree to switch places so that Pwyll can fight Annwn's opponent in the Otherworld. Magically they change into the appearance of each other and rule their opposite lands for one year.

In Annwn Pwyll finds a tremendous court. It is full of

beautiful women all dressed in silk, and it holds the best armed warband he had ever seen. When they feast they use the largest amounts of meat and drink, all held in glorious vessels of gold and jewels. Arawn's wife he also describes as the most beautiful, pleasant and delightful woman he has ever met. After Arawn's enemy is defeated by Pwyll a great friendship grows between the two rulers. Pwyll is then known as Head of Annwn and has a magical relationship with the Otherworld from then on.

Also in the Mabinogion is the tale of Branwen Daughter of Llyr. An army travels to Ireland led by the god Bran in order to avenge an insult to Branwen. The battle is won but at a great cost. Bran returns only as a magical head carried by his seven companions, the only survivors of the battle. They are instructed to go to Harlech in North Wales and there they enter the Otherworld. Food and drink are provided in abundance and they are entertained by the magical birds of Rhiannon who fly in Cardigan Bay.

Then they travel to Gwales in Penfro; reaching it they forget all their sorrow and suffering and stay there for many years in joy and delight as the Assembly of the Head. There were three doors there, one of which they were told not to open until the end of the assembly. When it is opened they re-enter the real world. All of their pain and suffering swiftly returns and they remember all the comrades they had lost in the battle with Ireland.

The stories of the famous Welsh poet Taliesin also describe the many pleasures of the Otherworld. In one poem Arthur goes to Annwn to bring back a magical

95

cauldron which provides an endless supply of food. Annwn is also described in the book as an island off the coast of Wales called Caer Sidi. It is a land of everlasting youth and a fountain exists there which pours forth a continuos torrent of food. The cauldron or fountain of plenty also appears in other Celtic tales about the Otherworld.

In the Irish tales the Otherworld survives less tainted by changes than in Wales. It is called The Land of Promise and The Land of Youth. The fairies are the *Sidhe* or *Tuatha De Danaan*, an ancient race of gods and goddesses who interact with the mortal heroes and the other Irish gods. They hold immense power and the Otherworld is the place where the sacred fountain and the nine hazelnuts of inspiration are found, great symbols of creation and the skill of poetry.

In the Otherworld nothing is what it appears to be. In a Celtic tale from Brittany we can see why the fairies were so angry with Elidorus for stealing the golden ball. In the story a hunter enters a cave and all the moss inside turns to gold. Lights illuminate the chamber and show a table piled high with food. The hunter eats but as he does so some golden skittles appear and are knocked down by a golden ball. The golden ball turns into a fairy who starts to sing beautifully. Elidorus, in his ignorance, had stole much more than mere riches, he had stolen one of the fairies themselves!

The tale of Elidorus was written about the same time as the Mabinogion. It is only the earlier sources of the Mabinogion that make its Lord of the Otherworld a fully grown man rather than Elidorus's knee-high king. As the tales of the gods and heroes became forgotten the Otherworld was kept alive in the popular folk stories of the fairies. The stories dealt less and less with battles and enchantments and more with moral tales of how greed and selfishness meant losing the pleasure of the Otherworld.

The fairies may have shrank in size with time but the people of Wales never forgot the sheer delight and beauty that the Otherworld promised. The Otherworld was the place where the ancient Celts believed they went after death and it became easily comparable with the Christian Heaven. Like Heaven it was a paradise, the sinful had no place there and only beauty and truth reigned. Because of this the Otherworld concept easily survived in the dreams of the people.

The transition from pagan to Christian religion was not always easy and smooth however. The next tale shows how the Celtic Otherworld was seen by the priests who first came to preach Christianity in Britain.

GWYN AP NUDD

This tale is not properly from Glamorgan but it has close links to a particular part of the county, namely the Vale of Neath. The legends concerning King Arthur, giants and fairies at Craig y Ddinas take place at the top of this vale and fairy stories, like that of Elidorus, abound in the region. Gwyn ap Nudd was the king of the Welsh fairies and was lord over the Otherworld where they lived. He is also a Celtic god and is linked to the Vale of Neath by his name of Nudd.

The legend itself comes from *The Life of St Collen*, preserved in a manuscript from 1536. He is the patron saint of Llangollen and lived in the sixth century, the time to which this story probably refers. When the saints first came to preach about God in the pagan lands of Britain they would have encountered the Celtic gods and goddesses in the minds of the people. As the head of the Celtic Otherworld Gwyn ap Nudd would have been an obvious target for the new Christian missionaries. This legend shows what happened when the two different religions met:

"St Collen was living in a cave as a hermit to be at peace with God. He lived frugally off the land and devoted all of his time to the Lord. Glad to be free of the distractions of the outside world he passed the time with prayer and meditation. One day while he was at prayer his peace and calm was broken by two people talking loudly below him. They were arguing about something and as Collen listened further, wishing they would leave him alone, he overheard one of the men invoke a name.

'By Gwyn ap Nudd who is lord over us all and holds all of Annwn in his sway,' were the words one of them spoke. Collen was angered for the man was talking about devils while he was trying to commune with his Lord.

'Leave this place!' he shouted out at them; 'hold your tongues and speak not of devils in the holy presence of God!'

The two men looked at each other with a bewildered expressions on their faces.

'You have courage to talk of our master in such a way hermit,' one of the men said. 'If others heard you talk in such a way you would not have the strength left to even open your mouth. We have noticed your presence here and the king whom you insult requests your company on the hill top at noon.

Then the men were gone and Collen was left to his prayers, having no intention of meeting anyone that day.

The next morning he heard the two men talking again and went to the mouth of the cave to listen.

'It is grim indeed that a man who claims to represent so much wisdom will not even accept an invitation from his host. Does he think he owns where he lives? Does he not think himself a guest in this land? The king asks his presence once more at noon, maybe this time he will not be so rude.'

Collen heard but ignored the men, he had more reason to stay and pray than he had to go and cavort with devils.

The next morning he was disturbed once again by the men talking loudly outside the cave.

'Our king will not wait forever. He kindly requests that you put away any hostilities that you have against him and come to his court to eat. He is eager to talk with you about your God and promises no harm will come to you. Once again he asks for your attendance this noon on the hill top'.

Collen was getting no rest with all these interruptions. To try and rid himself of these distractions he decided to accept the invitation.

'I will come,' he shouted, 'now begone!'

Later that day he prepared himself in his robe to meet the king, taking the precaution of carrying some holy water with him. Once he reached the hilltop he was dismayed to find nothing there. Moments later however a castle appeared and the air was filled with the noise of jovial celebration.

On the hilltop outside the castle stood lines of troops, looking strong and proud in their shining armour. Around them danced musicians playing flutes, harps, drums and all sorts of strange instruments. The music filled the air with beautiful melodic strains that floated around the exposed hilltop as if it were the wind itself.

Groups of people danced happily around the hill to the music. Brightly dressed youths formed rings and spun each other wildly around, occasionally letting go and flying off in all directions. Young men rode along the hilltop wearing shining cloaks of red, green and blue, their horses stepping along gracefully and proud. They were the most beautiful and graceful people that Collen had ever seen.

The court was so full of merriment and happiness that Collen thought they must be celebrating something very special. He walked through the throng and into the castle looking for the person who had invited him there. A brightly dressed courtier came to him and said that the king was waiting in the hall ready to begin a feast.

Once he entered the hall the king was there to greet him. He was seated on a bright golden throne that was covered with carved serpents. His eyes glittered a deep green and his blonde hair shone as bright as the rays of the sun. His face broke into a wide smile when he saw the saint approaching.

'Welcome to my court wise man,' he said to Collen in a deep booming voice, 'I am pleased that one so honourable as you chose to accept my invitation at last!'

'I chose to accept merely to rid myself of your peoples chatter and to get some peace,' the saint said.

'Did they annoy you?' The king laughed. 'Well no matter for you are here now. Everything you see here is also yours saint for I have not received one as wise as you for a long while. You may eat whatever food you see. I'm sure you will think it the finest you have ever tasted.

'I am not hungry,' the saint said, not looking too impressed with the king's feast.

'Well, you will drink then!' the king continued, 'Whatever we have here is yours to taste, mead, wine or liquor, you will never have tasted better nor will you find such quality ever again.'

'I am not thirsty either,' answered the saint.

'No matter!' laughed the king. 'You will receive the hospitality and service of the best of my people. They will entertain you with music, dancing and song, the best that you have ever heard or seen. Kings and both men and woman of rank wait to talk with you. To hold counsel with one so wise would be an honour for them. My whole kingdom is yours to wander through at will.'

'I do not wish to talk with anyone,' Collen replied. 'I do not wish to watch singing or dancing and neither do I wish to see any more of your kingdom.'

'You refuse everything I offer you! Do you not find this land a pleasant one? Does not the singing delight you or the host in their splendid armour fill you with awe?'

'The land and the songs are nice enough, king, but the host's armour shows me the true nature of this place,' answered Collen.

'How is that?'

'The armour is coloured red and blue, the red for the flames of hell and the blue for the coldness of this place,' said Collen.

With that the saint took out his vial of holy water and threw it around the court. The king disappeared along with the knights, musicians, singers, maidens and food and the

102

court was no more. Everything vanished and St Collen was left alone on the hilltop. The saint returned to his prayers and was not bothered by the fairies again".

The beliefs in Gwyn ap Nudd and his kind could not co-exist with the new religion of the saints that were making their faith known in Wales. Gwyn ap Nudd appears as a central figure in Welsh mythology, he is the Lord of the Dead and the Master of the Hunt. In folklore he becomes the king of the fairies but his original position was as a mighty warrior and huntsman who assembled the souls of the dead in Annwn. His name, Gwyn, and that of his father, Nudd, are easily recognised in the ancient name of the county of Gwynedd.

Gwyn also has an Irish parallel with Finn, a hero who ate the salmon of knowledge and became a great poet and warrior. His great great grandfather was a king of the Tuatha de Danaan who were a race of gods that later became fairies and was called Nuada 'of the silver arm'. Nudd was also called 'of the silver hand,' and the similarities between the two figures are numerous. They both seem to have been solar deities, the epithet of the silver arm or hand possibly relating to the rays of the sun.

Although their parentage is linked with the sun Gwyn and Finn are more associated with the earthy Otherworld of mortal death. The names Gwyn and Finn both mean fair or light but this is more an indication of the paradise that is the Otherworld. Death was not always associated with darkness as in our modern culture but with the bright afterlife of the Otherworld, a similar place to heaven.

103

This symbolism is evident in the legend of the combat between Gwyn and Gwythur ap Greidawl, 'Victor son of light' for Creudylad, daughter of Lludd. This battle happens every May-Day until the end of time and symbolises the contest between winter and summer in spring for the flowering earth. Gwyn is equated with the desolate winter and in the Black Book of Carmarthen he is thus described as a god of war and death.

Ederyn, another son of Nedd who is the Sparrowhawk Knight in the last story must have also had a place and function as a hero or god. These original tales do not survive, only his later role as a medieval knight has come down to us. The Irish stories that feature Finn are very numerous and it is through this instance of good survival that we can truly appreciate how many stories relating to Gwyn and Ederyn have been lost through the passage of time.

The connection between Gwyn ap Nudd and Neath is obvious. The main river running through the vale is called the river Nedd and the Welsh form is Castellnedd. The spelling variation of Nedd and Nudd is only a minor alteration that occurs with all languages as they develop through time; this change occurs also with the name of the county of Gwynedd. Nudd, if pronounced in Welsh, also gives the English Neath.

River names are the oldest forms of names and many survive unchanged or only a little altered from as far back as prehistory. Many rivers can be equated with known names of Celtic gods and goddesses, the Severn from the goddess Sabrann, the Boyne from the Irish goddess Boann and the Briant in Anglesey from the goddess **Brigantia**. The mother goddess Danu, a very important figure in Celtic mythology, has given her name to the Danube. In Wales Don, the equivalent of Danu, survives in the river names of Dyfrdonwy and Trydonwy.

The name of the river Nedd has parallels with the rivers Nidda and Nied in Germany and Nidd in Yorkshire. The word itself is related to the ancient British feminine word Nida but giving any meaning to the word Nedd is very difficult. It may mean shining river, relating to the Celtic word 'nid' meaning shining or bright, or it may not. Ascribing its origins to the god Nedd is plausible given the wealth of evidence from elsewhere. This raises the interesting point that as the rivers are all named after goddesses then Nudd may have once been female like the Irish goddess of death or had a consort with a similar name to his.

More evidence comes from a Glamorgan folk custom. On All Hallows Eve parties of young people would knock on doors asking for treats and singing short songs. This festival owes its existence to the earlier Celtic festival of the dead and one of the songs translates as: 'O Judy is dead and the corpse is in the grave, and her soul in a wheelbarrow going towards Neath'. The origins of most of these songs are lost as they are very obscure but what this song tells us has a lot of significance. All Hallows Eve and its Celtic predecessor was a time when the gates of the Otherworld were open to our world. The reference must be that the girl's soul was travelling to Gwyn's Otherworld domain in the Vale of Neath.

The main evidence is all so ancient and mostly

forgotten that we can never really know the true origins but the vale and river of Nedd does seem to be related to the god Nudd. The Vale of Neath may have once been considered as where this god and his son lived or originated from. Alternatively it was an easy point of entry into the Otherworld on account of its beauty. Folklore tales concerning the fairies are certainly numerous in the area. It is through clues such as the name of the river Nedd that we must turn to if we hope to reconstruct the ancient religion of the tribes that once lived in Wales.

THE SEASONAL
FESTIVALS

The festivals relating to the turn of the seasons throughout the year were very important in Celtic culture. With symbolic rituals and customs they marked the physical changes of the agricultural year. For a society that was heavily dependent on its crops and animals the end of one season and the beginning of another was a time to count their past blessings and protect their futures.

The four main Celtic festivals were known in Irish as Samhain, Oimelc, Beltane and Lughnasadh. They concerned the passage of life, death and growth that the different seasons gave to the land. Throughout the Celtic world from the Iron Age up to the present day they have been celebrated in similar ways. In Glamorgan some of the aspects of each of these festivals survived in the recorded folklore and folk customs of the last few centuries.

The festival of Samhain marked both the end and the

beginning of the year. It occurred on the full moon closest to the 1st November and the celebrations would last for three days and nights. Essentially these days existed out of normal time and it was a period when anything was possible. Divination and prophecies were more accurate if made at this time and were practised widely. The Otherworld was also closest at this time and spirits, gods and goddesses walked in the mortal world.

Many of the events in Irish myth involving the Otherworld occur at this magical time. Samhain was when the death goddess the Morrigu mated with the father god the Dagda to bring forth winter. The triple death described in the chapter on Twm also occurred in this time out of time. The five provinces of Ireland gathered at Tara, the ritual centre of Ireland, on Samhain. At this assembly there would be fairs, markets, contests and the affairs of the year would be discussed. It was a time of both death and birth and the festival was therefore both joyful and gloomy but it was always energetic.

This Celtic festival is what gave us the Christianised version of All Saints Day or Halloween on the 1st November and All Souls Day on the 2nd November. The Christian version of this pagan celebration still concerns the dead and instead of being a time when gods walked the earth it became a time to commemorate the Christian saints and the souls of the dead.

The reason why the Christian religion took this festival as its own was because people continued to celebrate the old pagan festival. It was easier for them to reinvent it as their own than it was to totally eradicate the pagan beliefs.

The survival of the Halloween customs of dressing up as witches or ghosts reflects how well the old beliefs survived up to modern times.

The Welsh name for this celebration is *Calan Gaeaf* or Winter Calend. The festival would start the previous night and it was the weirdest night of the year. The spirits were said to walk the earth on this night, the most famous of them being the *Ladi wen* or White Lady and the *Hwch Ddu Gwta* or Tailess Black Sow. It was the fear of this black sow that was partly behind the practice of lighting fires through the night.

The fires were also lit to mark a cleansing period after the old year had passed and the new one was about to begin. The bonfires were lit on the tops of hills throughout the country, many of them within sight of others. The celebrations would consist of singing, dancing and playing music around the fire while apples and potatoes were cooked and eaten. Each of the people present would throw a stone into the fire. If it was found in the morning it was a portent of a good year, if lost to the flames the year would bring misfortune.

When the fire started to die down everyone would run home shouting songs and poems warning of the Black Sow who represented the dark cold times to come. At home there would be drinking, feasting, storytelling, games of skill and also divination. As the old beliefs were that the Otherworld was closest to the real world on this night it was the best time for glimpsing into the future. The nights divination took many forms.

Nuts were thrown in the fire in a game called *Cnau*

mewn Llaw or Nuts in Hand. If they burned brightly they told of a good year if they did not they were a sign of death. Nuts were also burnt while making wishes, to tell whether a marriage would occur and to see if a partner had been faithful. I have already mentioned the magical hazelnut tree of wisdom that grew in the Otherworld. These divination games relate to the importance of the nut as a symbol of divine Otherworld wisdom.

Marriage games were an important part of the festival. A variety of divination methods were used to find a future partner. In Glamorgan there was a tradition that involved obtaining a pair of garters from a girl at the Halloween party. When they were tied in a lovers knot and placed under the skirt before going to sleep the partner would appear in a dream. Another method involved a couple placing two wheat grains on a shovel in a fire. If they jumped off together then the couple would be married, if not then they would separate in the year to come. Marriage was an important event for the young people and this night the spirits were active to assist them in making the right choice.

As the three day period was a time where anything was allowed, the boys and girls of Glamorgan used to swap their clothes around. Then they used to visit the neighbouring houses singing songs for the dead in return for small rewards. This cross-dressing was a widespread feature of the festival, the days that never existed being used for as much merriment as possible. In the times before our calendar came into effect it was also the start of the new year and so usually involved drinking and partying to excess.

The hag or death goddess is the figure mainly associated with this time of the year in Celtic myth. The feast on the night before the festival was sometimes called the hag's feast. This aspect has survived in the fears of the Black Sow and in the men's custom of dressing up in animal skins and rags. They pretended to be fearful hags or witches as they sung and danced their way around in return for coins or ale. This symbolised the death of the year as the old hag was the barrenness that was visiting everybodys home as winter descended on the earth.

Death was another important part of this Otherworld festival. Soul Cakes were baked for the dead and sold to families who gave them to their deceased. In nineteenth century Glamorgan a custom existed of reciting the lords prayer backwards around a churchyard while wearing your clothes on inside out. After this the porch of the church was entered and they would see the people who were about to die through the keyhole. The essential belief was that peoples' souls went to the Otherworld after death and so it would be easier to see the destinies of those who would soon be going there.

The February festival brought happier tidings. In Ireland it is called *Imbolc* or *Oimelc* and is celebrated on the 1st February. The name itself refers to the lactation of ewes in the lambing season and it was linked to Brigit, a mother goddess figure who presided over woman in childbirth. It was a festival mainly concerned with the approaching birth of the year and the fertility that was

111

beginning to show on the land.

This festival was mainly celebrated in Wales as part of the Christian celebration of Candlemass. The light of candles was the main feature of Mary's festival of the candles and they were carried in procession around the town or village. After the reformation the candles still remained as a symbol of the approaching spring and they were lit in the whole house to help the new season throw off the old.

The festival of Beltane on May the 1st marked the arrival of spring. The Irish name for the festival means goodly fire and it was a celebration of the renewal of life in the summer months. Fires were lit on hills and in the fields to assist and welcome the suns return. Cattle were driven between two lit fires to cleanse them of disease before they were let out to pasture in the fields. In the ninth century Irish source of Cormac's Glossary this was said to have been done under the auspices of the Druids.

The god Belennus, a solar and healing deity was probably linked with these rituals. House fires were extinguished and then relit from the bonfire to cleanse the house of the old fire of the winter. The ashes of the fire were sometimes scattered on the fields or mixed with next year's seed corn. Branches of the sacred tree were also given to each household to be burnt to help the general well-being of the family and their harvest.

There were sacrificial aspects to the lighting of the summer fires. In some areas horse skulls and bones were thrown on the fire, in Perthshire cakes were picked from a bag and the taker of the burnt cake was seen as chosen and thrown in the fire. Although death did not occur in this instance it may be seen as a remnant of an earlier custom where a sacrifice was actually made to the sun. It could also have originated simply as a symbolic sacrifice as there is no direct evidence for human sacrifice at this time.

The May king and queen were chosen as human representatives of the summer. They represented the sexual partnership that brings growth and fertility to the land after the death of winter. The May pole was the centre of the May festivities and it may have its origins in the sacred tree of the tribe. The tree certainly represented the vegetation spirit or god and the people honoured this deity by dancing around the May pole. Sometimes the Beltane fire was lit beneath the sacred tree itself or the tree was eventually burnt whole on the fire.

In Wales the night before the Calan Haf or Summer Calend was considered one of the *ysbrydnos* or spirit nights when the dead roamed the land. Bonfires were lit on this night, the last of which is recorded to have been kindled in the 1830s. One interesting recorded custom was when nine men collected nine different kinds of tree sticks. After this was done they would cut a circle in the grass, set the wood around the circle and light the fire with two oak sticks. This custom sounds very old as the number nine has always had the utmost importance in a lot of Celtic countries and appears regularly in Celtic mythology.

The sacrificial elements of the festival are also evident. As in Perthshire cakes were chosen from a bag and the recipient of the odd one would have to leap screaming over

113

the fire to ensure a good harvest. If there were disease within the herd a calf or sheep would be thrown into the flames in an effort to cleanse the rest of the herd. The Irish custom of driving the cattle between two fires is also found in Wales. After this was considered too cruel, the cattle were driven over the ashes of the fire. The ashes of the Beltane fire were held in the highest regard. They were collected to protect homes against disease or if they were sprinkled in shoes they protected the wearer from harm.

In Glamorgan this was the time of the *Taplas Haf* when the town met at the village green. A harpist or fiddler played and the people took part in games and contests. The May pole activities in Glamorgan were however secondary to the midsummer festival. This celebration of the longest day of summer was Christianised into St John the Baptist Day. The Celtic midsummer festival was celebrated in almost the same way as the Beltane festivals in that fires and trees were the main elements.

The Summer birch was raised in Glamorgan on the eve before midsummer. It was usually trimmed and decorated with coloured ribbons, wreaths and pictures. One raised in Wenvoe in the mid eighteenth century was decorated by young girls and topped with a weathercock covered in ribbons. The birch tree had to be protected at this time as it was customary for towns to try and topple each other's trees.

The diary of William Thomas recorded an event in Cardiff in 1768 where the people of the parish of St Fagans were protecting their birch with guns from fifty people of St Nicholas parish. When St Nicholas recruited more people from their area St Fagans called on people from all around Llandaff and Cardiff to help them. It was a sign of great disgrace for a parish if they lost their birch tree and they could not raise another until they stole someone elses.

The birch, or painted wooden god as the above writer called it, was used for dancing around and was the central piece of the festivities. Divination was also practised on this night and St John's Wort was collected at noon and placed over the doors to purify the houses. If the plant was dug at midnight it was also useful for driving witches away. This usage of the plant is very probably pre-Christian and is an integral part of the protective nature of the festivities at the important time of crop growth.

The last festival of the Celtic year was *Lughnasadh*, the harvest festival that has been Christianised into Lammas. It was primarily a time of giving thanks for the year's harvest. In Irish mythology it originated from the god Lug whose foster mother Tailtu died and was buried on the day. He proclaimed that a fair should be held on the day to honour his mother and to celebrate his marriage. The partner of Lug was Erin, the sovereignty of Ireland, symbolising the unity of the gods with the land.

Great feasts were held with the abundance of food available at this time. The last sheafs of corn from the harvest were ceremoniously cut. These sheafs represented the hag and the maiden, the spirits of the harvested crop and the crop of the year to come. They were given as feed to the cattle or mixed in with next years seeds to ensure a continuity of good luck for the forthcoming year. Similar

115

traditions exist all over Europe at this time of the year and the festival must be very ancient.

Marriages were arranged and it was a time of happiness and love making so that the children could be born the next spring to coincide with the festival of Brigit the god of women in childbirth. It was a feminine festival as the women were important in the harvesting of the crop. Fertility was an important part of the corn spirit customs and nudity would have been used to portray this fecundity.

In Glamorgan and the rest of Wales this festival marked the end of the hard work of crop growing and harvesting. All of the farmers and workers would get together to feast and to reap the *Caseg Fedi*. The *Caseg Fedi* was the harvest mare or the last sheaf of corn. The sheaf would be plaited in the field and the workers would take it in turns to try and cut it off from a distance. Whoever cut the sheaf would sing a rhyme and try and get it into the farmhouse untouched while the woman tried to wet it with water. If he succeeded the sheaf would be hung up to dry and he would hold prime place at the dinner table. This last sheaf was believed to hold the corn spirit and the forces of growth and was kept in the house as a good luck charm.

These festivals were of prime social importance among agricultural communities in Wales. The customs and traditions were honoured year after year to bring good fortune and to give thanks for past fortunes. As the customs and traditions were so deeply rooted in the minds and societies of the Welsh communities these traditions are perhaps the most ancient in this book. Legends must have been told at the festivities that mirrored the seasons, like that of Gwyn ap Nudd and Gwythur ap Greidawl which represented the battle of winter and summer over spring, but these important stories like so many others have been forgotten.

CONCLUSION

The legends in this book represent almost all the stories of length concerning Glamorgan that remain. There are however hundreds of other fragments of folklore and myth that exist in written sources and in place names. These pieces can be used to give deeper meaning to the Celtic culture of Glamorgan but are dealt with sufficiently in other books.

I hope these legends have enabled the reader to glimpse back to the time when these stories were alive in people's minds and mouths. They are an important part of Glamorgan's past and show that to experience the wonders and mystery of Celtic legends you need not look further than your own local area. The secrets of the past are everywhere and just need to be searched for to be discovered. There is much more work to be done in Glamorgan and the rest of Wales to piece together these remnants of Celtic mythology. I hope this book has introduced the richness of what is to be found. I also hope it has made you think of the majestic feet that once walked across our native soil and the strange gods and fairies who are probably still out there somewhere.

BIBLIOGRAPHY

Bromwich, R, and Jarman, A (eds.), 'The Arthur of the Welsh', Cardiff, University of Wales Press, 1991.

Cross, T, and Slover, C, 'Ancient Irish Tales', Figgis, Dublin, 1936.

Berresford Ellis, P, 'The Druids', Constable, London, 1994.

Evans-Wentz, W.Y. 'The Fairy Faith In Celtic Countries', Colin Smythe, Gerrards Cross,1977 reprint.

Green, Miranda J, 'Dictionary of Celtic Myth and Legends', Thames & Hudson, London, 1992.

'The Mabinogion', trans. Jones, Gwyn & Thomas, Dent, London, 1978.

Macculloch, J.A. 'The Religion Of The Ancient Celts', Constable, London, 1992 reprint.

Morgan, A, 'Legends of Porthcawl and the Glamorgan Coast', D. Brown and Sons Ltd, Bridgend and Cowbridge, 1974.

Owen, Elias, 'Welsh Folklore', Oswestry and Wrexham, 1887.

Owen, Trefor, M. 'Welsh Folk Customs', National Museum of Wales, Cardiff, 1959.

Parry-Jones, D, 'Welsh Legends', Batsford, London, 1953.

Rhys, J. 'Celtic Folklore: Welsh and Manx', University Press, Oxford, 1901.

Rolleston, T.W. 'Celtic Myths and Legends', Bracken Books, London, 1986 reprint.

Sikes, Witr, 'British Goblins: The Realm of Faerie', Llanerch reprint, Felinfach, 1991.

Stewart, R.J., 'Celtic Gods and Goddesses', Blanford, London, 1990.

Williams, Gwyn, A., 'When Was Wales?' Penguin, London, 1985.